581 7

MW01121399

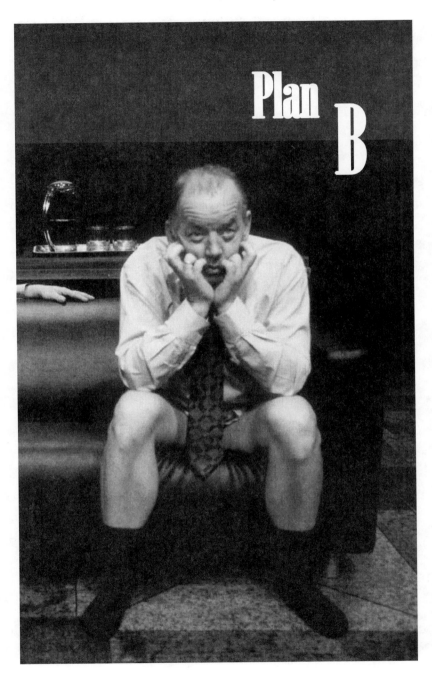

Plan B

Plan B

by
Michael Healey

Playwrights Canada Press
Toronto • Canada

Playwrights Canada Press
54 Wolseley Street, 2nd Floor
Toronto, Ontario CANADA M5T 1A5
416-703-0013   fax 416-703-0059   info@puc.ca   http://www.puc.ca

Playwrights Canada Press acknowledges the support of the taxpayers of Canada through The Canada Council for the Arts and the Ontario Arts Council.

Cover photo of Peter Donaldson (front) and John Dolan (back) by Cylla von Tiedemann.
Production Editor: Jodi Armstrong

National Library of Canada Cataloguing in Publication Data

Healey, Michael
    Plan B

A play.
ISBN 0-88754-641-2

    I. Title.

PS8565.E14P53 2002   C812'.54   C2002-900196-X
PR9199.3.H396P53 2002

First edition: April 2002.
Printed and bound by AGMV Marquis at Quebec, Canada.

For Urjo, with gratitude.

ACKNOWLEDGEMENTS

Urjo Kareda committed to the play after seeing about 14 pages of material. His belief in the show sometimes outweighed my own. My thanks to Andy McKim and the members of the Tarragon Playwright's Unit of 2000, as well as the actors who read the play during workshops: Randy Hughson, Waneta Storms, Ron White, David Jansen, Paul Gross, Martha Burns, Ken James, Marie-Helene Fontaine and Dennis O'Connor.

The three weeks I spent at the Banff Centre in the summer of 2000 turned out to be critical, so my thanks to Bob White, Paula Dankert and all of the actors who read the script during that time.

Thanks finally to the Shaw Festival, which co-produced *Plan B*'s first production, and where the script underwent workshops in 2000 and 2001.

Plan B was first produced at the Tarragon Theatre, Toronto, in co-production with the Shaw Festival, in January of 2002, with the following cast:

Peter Donaldson   Michael Fraser
John Dolan   Mathieu Lapointe
Marie-Helene Fontaine   Lise Frechette
Peter MacNeill   Colin Patterson

Directed by Richard Greenblatt
Set designed by Glen Charles Landry
Costumes designed by Christina Poddubiuk
Lighting design by Andrea Lundy
French translation by Sonya Malaborza
Stage Managed by Randa Doche

CHARACTERS

MICHAEL Fraser
MATHIEU Lapointe
LISE Frechette
COLIN Patterson

PLAYWRIGHT'S NOTE

The italicized dialogue in this script is to be spoken in French.

PROLOGUE

The ballroom of a hotel in Hull. A huge table, with a pitcher of water surrounded by upturned glasses at its centre; chandelier above. Four chairs. Doors right and left; stage right door leads to the Quebec war room, stage left door to the Canadian war room.

Before house lights go down, the Quebec door opens, and LISE Fréchette, Intergovernmental Affairs Minister, mid-forties, enters. Extremely classy suit, with one extraordinary accessory, perhaps in the footwear realm. She waits. She strolls the room, and underneath her ordered demeanour, we may or may not be able to discern a certain ebullience.

The Canadian door opens, and Senator COLIN Patterson enters. 60 years old, crumbed and soup-spotted, senator from Saskatchewan. LISE whirls around, and then approaches him. They shake hands. They leave by their respective doors. Pause.

The Quebec door opens, and LISE returns with MATHIEU Lapointe, Premier Ministre of Quebec. Late fifties, classy dresser. Upon entering the room and discovering it empty, he gives LISE a look of inquiry. LISE is forced to shrug. He heads for the door, and LISE opens it. MATHIEU exits.

Eventually the Canadian door opens and COLIN enters followed by MICHAEL Fraser, Federal Finance Minister. Mid-forties, okay dresser in the tradition of English Canadian politicians. Which is to say, wardrobe selection is made with the subliminal intent of avoiding detection during question period. He smiles at LISE, who does not respond, but instead leaves through the Quebec door, leaving it open. House light has slowly faded down by this point, and "Cordelia" by the Tragically Hip begins. MICHAEL and COLIN regard the open door. MICHAEL looks at COLIN, who frowns. MICHAEL moves toward the Quebec door. The door swings open and LISE and MATHIEU re-enter, and MICHAEL transforms his move with

*the intention of snooping into a warm cross, the
point of which is to shake hands with Mathieu.
They shake hands. MICHAEL shakes LISE's hand;
MATHIEU shakes COLIN's. LISE and COLIN
pointlessly shake hands again.*

*MICHAEL and MATHIEU take seats at the table,
and LISE and COLIN place leather folders before
their respective bosses. They seat themselves in
chairs slightly away from the table, handy to the
men they serve. A beat, and then the lights slowly
fade down. Blackout.*

*The lights snap up on this tableau: The men have all
risen from their chairs; COLIN has moved forward
and is leaning across the table at MATHIEU,
MICHAEL and MATHIEU are shocked. LISE sits
with her hand over her mouth. COLIN is breathing
hard. The music snaps off, and then:*

COLIN   *(to MATHIEU)* You're a bit of a FUCKIN'
ASSHOLE, AREN'T YOU?

*What he says is translated into French and projected
above the stage. Blackout. The music resumes at a
higher level.*

ACT I

SCENE ONE

> *The ballroom. COLIN stands, the others sit.*
> *Everything everyone says in English is translated*
> *into French and projected above the stage;*
> *everything said in French is translated into English*
> *and projected below it. The music fades out.*

COLIN   *(who looks first at the ceiling and then at his fingernails)*
...never my intention to sour the first day's
proceedings with that sort of, uh, outburst. Let me
say that I realize that Mr. Fraser here, as ranking
Federal Minister is our lead on this, and that I am
only meant to be his silent council here in the
negotiating room. So my apology extends not only
to you, Mr. Lapointe, but also to you, Michael;
I'm, uh, sorry. And finally to you, Ms Fréchette,
I apologize for the cursing. As the woman in the
room.

LISE   *That's not necessary.*

COLIN   *(A beat while he translates her statement in his head)*
Uh, thank you very much.

     COLIN sits.

MICHAEL   Thank you, Colin. I think we can all agree that
what we are attempting to accomplish here is best
pursued without passions, if at all possible. These
are delicate negotiations, as we are all aware, and
we will only make headway, I think, if we can
manage to keep our feelings in check.

MATHIEU   Yes.

MICHAEL   Yes. You have my apology as well, Monsieur
Lapointe, and in an effort to get this off on the
right foot, I commit to having a written version
of Colin's apology delivered to your people by
noon tomorrow.

MATHIEU   Thank you.

MICHAEL   Not at all.

LISE   Well, if we've finished with, um, all of that,
            I suggest we proceed with the joint opening
            communiqué.

MICHAEL   All right.

LISE   As you know, after the release of the communiqué,
            we will impose a news blackout until the comple-
            tion of the talks.

MICHAEL   Yes, the news blackout. Have we finalized a leak
            schedule?

LISE   Yes.

            LISE and COLIN hand their bosses a piece of paper
            each.

MICHAEL   Ah. Yes. *(to MATHIEU)* Nothing like a regularly
            scheduled leak to keep things running smoothly.

            MATHIEU looks at MICHAEL.

            Ha ha.

MATHIEU   *(after a beat, holding up the leather folder)* Here is our
            proposal for the joint opening communiqué.

MICHAEL   Right. And here's ours.

MATHIEU   Shall we look these over to see if there's enough
            common ground to begin work on a mutually
            agreeable version?

            They exchange folders.

MICHAEL   Absolutely. Reconvene tomorrow, 10AM?

MATHIEU   All right.

MICHAEL   Good. *(extends his hand to MATHIEU)* Good first
            day.

MATHIEU   *(already on his way out of the room, he does not see MICHAEL's hand)* Yes.

           LISE sees MICHAEL left hanging. She exits.

MICHAEL   Okay. Good. See ya. Well. That went good, I thought.

COLIN   Fuckin' prick.

MICHAEL   Yeah. She seems nice, though.

COLIN   Treasonous bastard.

MICHAEL   Yes, Colin, you're good at your job.

COLIN   Eh?

MICHAEL   The grumpy old loose cannon. The righteous defender of what we used to call a Dominion. You can stop now. They're out of the room.

COLIN   Yeah. Well. It happens to be how I really feel.

MICHAEL   What?

COLIN   Sure. The guy's a douchebag. He lied to all those people for two fuckin' years, scared the living shit out of them until they–

MICHAEL   Hold on. Wait a minute. I don't know if I want someone in here with me who's actually feeling things.

COLIN   Too friggin' bad.

MICHAEL   But–

COLIN   Hey. Tell me something. You gonna make a peepee joke every time someone uses the word "leak?" I just wanna know, because if you are, I think I'm gonna–

MICHAEL	Okay, okay. Jeez. I was just trying to inject a little levity into the proceedings. I mean, Christ, it's not like we're doing some momentous thing here.
COLIN	Nonetheless. Let's try to remember we're meant to be adults.
MICHAEL	What about you? We're not in the room ten minutes, you're calling the guy names. You're going to have to control yourself.
COLIN	Who says.
MICHAEL	Aw, c'mon, Colin. There's a plan, and we agreed to the plan, about how the next two weeks are going to go. I mean, how often was I told "nothing unplanned will actually occur in the room."
COLIN	It wasn't.
MICHAEL	What.
COLIN	Unplanned. It was planned.
MICHAEL	Oh yeah? Whose plan.
COLIN	Ours. Our plan included my outburst and your not being apprised of its inclusion in our plans.
MICHAEL	Ho. Wait a minute. I won't do this if I only know part of the plan.
COLIN	Sorry?
MICHAEL	I mean, well, I'd prefer to know the whole plan, okay?
COLIN	Sorry.
MICHAEL	Well, shit.
COLIN	Michael. If this were the real negotiation, you'd know the whole plan, okay? If this mattered, you'd be in on the whole thing. But because this is all

planned, we thought it would be good for some unplanned stuff to happen. My outburst, which you handled correctly by the way, lent an air of the chaotic to what is in reality a heavily choreographed exercise.

MICHAEL Okay.

COLIN Can I just point out that any status you gained by handling me correctly, you lost at the end when you stood there with your dick out?

MICHAEL Yeah, okay.

COLIN So.

MICHAEL Yeah.

COLIN Don't do that.

MICHAEL Okay. So at any time over the next two weeks, from now until we walk out, you could at any time go berserk, and I'm supposed to what, just handle it?

COLIN Yup.

MICHAEL You know, I've never been comfortable with spontaneity.

COLIN Aw, come on.

MICHAEL Not a big improviser. It's not my strength.

COLIN It's fun.

Blackout.

Scene Two

The ballroom. LISE and MATHIEU.

MATHIEU *When do they walk out?*

LISE   *End of next week.*

MATHIEU   *What over?*

LISE   *They're not sure. Federal lands, I think. They're getting back to us on that. Here's the latest on the real negotiations (hands him paper); they're now saying the agreement should be done by August, at which time we can stage another one of these meetings to ratify it.*

              MATHIEU reads.

              Hey. What are you doing later?

MATHIEU   *Later?*

LISE   *Yeah. I realized yesterday I have no desire to sit around the hotel room all night. I get antsy. You want to get a drink later?*

MATHIEU   *I don't think so.*

LISE   *Something to eat?*

MATHIEU   *I'm still not eating. Is everything all right?*

LISE   *I just, I don't feel like being there in the room. I find I want to get out. Don't you find that?*

MATHIEU   *Actually, I find that after spending two years doing what we've been doing, I welcome a quiet night in.*

LISE   *I would have thought that after galvanizing the public in the way that we did, you'd want to be out among them.*

MATHIEU   *You're funny. That's also why I'm looking forward to the next couple of weeks. Nice to be engaged in talks that don't actually amount to anything. It's a relief. It's a kind of vacation.*

LISE   *If and when I do take a vacation, it won't be in Hull, I assure you. So? Dinner later? C'mon. I know a place.*

MATHIEU   *Oh, no, I don't think so.*

The Canadians enter. MATHIEU hands the paper back to LISE.

MICHAEL   Good morning.

MATHIEU   Good morning.

LISE   Good morning.

COLIN   Good morning.

MICHAEL   Good morning. Well. We've had a look at your proposal for the opening communiqué, and we found many areas of common, of, common, of commonality between it and ours. We think we should be able to speed through to a resolution on it, and get the communiqué to the press in short order.

MATHIEU   Good.

MICHAEL   Did you have any thoughts on ours?

MATHIEU   Well...

LISE   No.

MICHAEL   No?

MATHIEU   No?

LISE   No. We didn't read yours.

MICHAEL   You didn't?

LISE   No. The document you gave us was in English.

MICHAEL   Oh.

COLIN   Aw, for fuck's sake...

MICHAEL   Hey! Colin! I apologize. Colin, will you please get a translated version of our opening communiqué? If one doesn't exist, then get one translated.

COLIN   Certainly. Translated into...?

MICHAEL   Thank you Colin.

                COLIN mutters obscenities on his exit.

MICHAEL   Shall we make it a practice, then, to give you everything in French?

LISE   Thank you, yes.

MICHAEL   Fine. Um. We'd like ours in English.

                LISE and MATHIEU share a little laugh.

MATHIEU   Certainly.

                A pause.

MICHAEL   Well, shall we just, uh, begin? As long as we're just sitting here, what about kicking some stuff around?

LISE   Do you think that's wise? Without Colin here?

MICHAEL   Well, look at the alternatives. We really can't adjourn early because we adjourned early yesterday. So either we talk about something, or we just sit here quietly and do nothing.

MATHIEU   Do you have any areas you think we might discuss?

MICHAEL   I thought we'd start with something gentle, something easy, like aboriginals. Or a southern passage to the Maritimes. Either of those grab you?

MATHIEU   Do you have anything written down?

MICHAEL   Well, no, I just thought we could, you know, kick it around, see if there's any basis for a discussion. Not that we'd be having a discussion, of course–

LISE   I don't think that's wise, do you?

MICHAEL   Federal lands?

LISE   Oh, it's too soon for that, don't you think? Isn't that
            the end of next week?

MICHAEL   Well, yes, but–

LISE   Don't want to get there prematurely.

MICHAEL   No, I, ha ha.

            A silence.

LISE   *(rapidly, to MATHIEU) Well, that stopped the poor
            dumb bastard cold.*

MATHIEU   *(glancing at MICHAEL) I'm sorry?*

LISE   *It's okay. If you talk fast enough, he doesn't understand.
            He's had two years of the course they give cabinet
            ministers.*

MATHIEU   *You mean the tapes for your car?*

LISE   *Yes. Ever hear him during question period? He speaks
            phon-et-ic-al-ly.*

MATHIEU   *I see. Um, what are you doing? I actually was prepared
            to discuss their version of the press release.*

LISE   *I know, I just, I felt like doing that. I don't know what's
            gotten into me.*

MATHIEU   *Are you going to behave like this for the next two weeks?
            Because I don't know if I–*

LISE   *I don't know. No. Sorry. Sorry. I'm just antsy.*

MATHIEU   *Let's just stick to the agenda, shall we?*

LISE   *Sure. Of course. Sorry.*

            A pause. LISE gets up and walks around.

LISE	*How have you been sleeping?*
MATHIEU	*I sleep fine.*

LISE *Because I don't sleep. I don't seem to need it. Since the night. I just need less. I feel like, don't you feel extraordinary?*

MATHIEU *Well, there's a lot of things to occupy me. I don't spend a lot of time thinking about how I feel.*

LISE *I don't either. But I can't seem to help it. All through the day, I walk around feeling all revved up. Like I could do anything. Feeling like I'm twice my size. That I could walk down the street, picking up cars, tossing them over my shoulder, that I could just stomp around doing anything I want. I can do anything I want. I could, I don't know...*

She looks at MICHAEL, smiles.

I could swallow that one whole.

MICHAEL smiles back.

Blackout.

Scene Three

The ballroom. All four present. LISE is reading.

LISE ...the purpose of which is to facilitate the creation of the fully autonomous state of Quebec.

MICHAEL Yes, and then I think we can drop in your paragraph about the timetable for the talks right there–

COLIN Paragraphe numéro sept.

MICHAEL Yes, Colin. And then I propose we follow with a merged version of your paragraph three and our paragraph eleven.

COLIN   Trois et onze.

MICHAEL   Thank you Colin, yes. Go ahead.

COLIN   Bon. "Due to the obviously sensitive nature of these discussions, and due to the unavoidable scrutiny the process will be under nationally and internationally; due as well to the potential for volatility in global trade, securities and currency exchanges as a result of incomplete or inaccurate reporting; and in an attempt to minimize the negative effects of unsubstantiated rumour or speculation; the principles agree that the talks will take place under a complete news blackout. Said blackout will remain in place until the completion of the talks, at which time a report will be issued, and joint and or more probably separate news conferences scheduled."

LISE   I beg your pardon?

MATHIEU   I would describe that as an inelegant merger of two formerly distinct and elegant paragraphs.

LISE   *(to COLIN, asking for the paper)* May I?

COLIN   Be my guest.

LISE   Well, how about this: "Because of the extraordinary circumstances that surround this historic negotiation, no releases to the press will be made until its completion."

MICHAEL   Well that's... I like it. Did you just do that? Off the top of your head?

LISE   Well, yes.

MICHAEL   Wow. Have we met?

LISE   I'm sorry?

MICHAEL   Nothing. Never mind.

COLIN	I object to the word "historic."
MICHAEL	You do?
MATHIEU	Can you suggest a substitute?
COLIN	"Despicable?"
MICHAEL	Colin…
COLIN	Or "treasonous?"
MICHAEL	Okay, Colin–
COLIN	How 'bout "treasonous prick bastard?"
MICHAEL	Hey! *(to MATHIEU)* We accept your wording, and I think that takes care of the joint opening communiqué. Shall we quit for the day now, get the thing printed up and then release it to the press?
MATHIEU	Seems a good idea.
MICHAEL	Good.

> COLIN *storms out of the room, MATHIEU exits. LISE gathers papers and MICHAEL lingers by the door.*

	…Sorry?
LISE	…Mr. Fraser?
MICHAEL	Did you speak?
LISE	No.
MICHAEL	Ah. That's probably wise.
LISE	It's…?
MICHAEL	Never mind.
LISE	All right.

MICHAEL	No no. Shhhh.
LISE	…Okay.
MICHAEL	No! Shhhh! The walls have, uh, uh… *(He nods.)*
LISE	*(looking around)* Wallpaper?
MICHAEL	Hah, ha haha ha hahahaha!

> *He takes a credit card out of his pocket, whizzes it across the room at her. It lands on the table. He indicates that she should take it. She does. He leaves.*
>
> *Blackout.*

Scene Four

> *MICHAEL's hotel room. He sits, watching the TV. He has removed his jacket and pants, and has loosened his tie. There is a noise at the door. He jumps up. The door opens and LISE, who has successfully figured out the credit card-type door key, steps in. A pause, while they regard each other.*

MICHAEL	Hello.
LISE	Uh huh.
MICHAEL	You figured out my subtle, uh, signal.
LISE	I did. It had the slightly icky appearance of a rehearsed move.
MICHAEL	Really? Wow.

> *A pause.*

MICHAEL	Um, it wasn't.
LISE	Would you mind turning that off?

MICHAEL   I suppose not. *(as he hunts for the remote)* Quebec
          City. 1992. The pre-G7 conference. The pointless
          conference. I was… nobody, yet. You strode in,
          fresh from throwing away the newspaper column
          for politics. You had on a suit that needed no blouse
          and it was this unbelievable shade of grey. And
          green shoes, with a heel. You got up, you spoke.
          It was your coming out party, that conference.
          (turns off the TV) And you talked right at me. Do
          you remember?

LISE   Of course.

MICHAEL   Did you talk right at me?

LISE   Of course not.

          A pause.

MICHAEL   You seem different.

LISE   I should hope so.

          A pause.

MICHAEL   You seem… I don't know…

LISE   Ebullient?

MICHAEL   Yes.

LISE   Well. Duh.

          A pause.

          Are you telling me you've been fascinated with me
          since 1992?

MICHAEL   Oh, God, no. I wouldn't say that.

LISE   I see.

MICHAEL   Should I say that?

LISE No. It's to your credit you don't.

MICHAEL Good. I get credit.

> *A pause.*

Sorry. Would you like a drink?

LISE Do you have any gin?

MICHAEL Uh, I have some Scotch.

LISE No, thank you.

MICHAEL Ah. Would you like to sit down?

LISE Would I like to sit down.

MICHAEL Yes.

LISE I, I think not.

MICHAEL I see. And yet, you've come.

LISE Yes. I have.

MICHAEL Yes.

LISE I…

MICHAEL Yes?

LISE I've come to give you this.

> *She hands him his room key.*

MICHAEL I see. Thank you.

LISE Yes. Well.

> *They look at each other.*

MICHAEL Um. Thanks a lot.

LISE	All right.

> *She goes. MICHAEL puts the room key in his shirt pocket, sits, turns the TV back on.*
>
> *Blackout.*

Scene Five

> *The ballroom; everyone in their places.*

MICHAEL	...Sorry?
COLIN	*(holding out paper)* It's today's leak. Take it.

> *MICHAEL takes the leak, and, reading, walks around the room. He pauses when he is directly behind LISE.*

MICHAEL	Uh huh. Uh huh. Ha ha. Huh. Well. This is some leak. This is a really, really – whose work is this?
LISE	It's mine.
MICHAEL	I might have guessed. This is one, uh, elusive leak. Vague and not vague at the same time. This leak is masterful, it's tantalizing: it'll get them worked up, but leave them wondering.
COLIN	Good. Okay. Now–
MICHAEL	This is, you know what this is? It's restrained, sure, but underneath, this leak is, is ebullient. And fascinating. I have been fascinated with this leak since I first laid eyes on it.
COLIN	Yes, Michael, I like it too, now can we–
MICHAEL	And yet, what am I to make of this leak? What is the message it's given me? If you had to summarize the leak's content, how would you do it?
COLIN	Well fer Christ's sake, it says that–

MICHAEL   I am really, really not asking you. *(to LISE)* What would you say is the actual message to be gleaned from this leak at this time?

LISE   Well, I think, in essence, its message is that the potential for further developments exists, and that they may in fact be imminent.

MICHAEL   Ah hah. Yes. Further developments. It's essentially a message of hope, then.

LISE   Yes. Hope of sorts. The main thing is to be prepared.

MICHAEL   Ah. I see. I commit fully to the spirit of this leak. You may consider me 100% solid on today's outstanding leak.

COLIN   Great. Okay.

MICHAEL   Let my unwavering commitment to today's leak never be in doubt.

LISE   Yes.

MICHAEL   And, in the spirit of preparation, let me say that I also commit fully to the gin issue.

COLIN   Tremendous. Whatever. Can we continue?

MICHAEL   *(to LISE)* Yes. May we continue?

LISE   By all means.

MICHAEL   Great.

> *MICHAEL takes the room key out of a pocket, and waves it around throughout the following.*

MICHAEL   So. What's today?

COLIN   Today we discuss debt.

MICHAEL   Right. *(to MATHIEU)* Well? What do you think?

MATHIEU   Uh…

COLIN   No, that's us. We start. You have the notes.

MICHAEL   Oh. Right. Where did I…. Oh well. Never mind.
           Um. It's a funny conversation, of course, given that
           we haven't sorted out the whole currency thing,
           but, uhhh, okay: We think that Quebec, as one of
           the two founding peoples, should take half the
           Federal debt when it goes.

MATHIEU   …Half?

COLIN   No, that's–

MICHAEL   Yes. It's a goodwill gesture. A country needs a debt
           these days, and your little provincial one isn't going
           to cut it out there.

COLIN   What are you–

MICHAEL   A portion of a country's bureaucracy depends on
           building and maintaining the debt. A portion of its
           citizenry. A portion of its economy. A country needs
           a big ol' debt, and I say take half of ours, and God
           bless.

MATHIEU   Are you serious?

COLIN   No, he's not, he's just–

MICHAEL   Hey. Look at me. Talk to me. That's our position on
           the debt.

MATHIEU   Um, that's not what my notes said you were going
           to say.

MICHAEL   Oh, well.

MATHIEU   Well, it's very interesting. Let me think about it,
           and I'll get back to you. It's a talk I'd enjoy having.

MICHAEL   Great. Now we're getting somewhere.

COLIN	Fuck are you doing?
MICHAEL	Am I not fulfilling our obligation to these talks by making that proposal instead of the scripted one? Given that we all know where the real decision about this stuff is being made?
COLIN	The real decision should look at least a little bit like what's coming out of this room. You get that, right? You get that part of the plan?
MICHAEL	I guess so, I just, I thought I'd improvise.

> *He flings the room key at LISE. It lands on the table before her.*

MICHAEL	I thought I'd make an unrehearsed move. Everybody seems interested in seeing me do some totally unplanned stuff.
COLIN	You need to shut up.
MICHAEL	Sorry. It was the leak. *(to the Quebecois) It was the leak. I lost my head.*

> *Blackout.*

SCENE SIX

> *MICHAEL's hotel room. He is pantless. The TV is on. LISE stands at the door, holding the room key.*

MICHAEL	It was the leak. I lost my head.
LISE	Not at all. Debt happens to be one of my favourite subjects.
MICHAEL	No way.
LISE	Seriously.
MICHAEL	Okay, but if you don't mind, I'm gonna pretend you're not serious about that.

LISE	No, I understand.
	A pause.
MICHAEL	He's an interesting guy, your boss. He seems, I don't know, so certain about everything.
LISE	That's because he is.
MICHAEL	No, but I mean, really. Like he has a watertight opinion about every single thing. And he doesn't just come across like he does, he, he comes across like he does.
LISE	He has the momentum of history behind him.
MICHAEL	Yeah. Ha ha. Holy shit, imagine if that were true.
	A pause.
	I'd invite you in, but that didn't workout so good last time.
LISE	No. It didn't, did it.
MICHAEL	And this is fun. Me here, you there. Nobody moving.
LISE	Uh huh.
	A pause.
	Do you, you seem to hate your pants.
MICHAEL	I have always hated my pants. I don't know why.
LISE	I see.
MICHAEL	First things off through the door.
	A pause.
LISE	But you like the television.

MICHAEL	Oh yeah. Big fan of the television. You're fantastic.

A pause.

Sorry. Would you like a drink?

LISE	I…
MICHAEL	Would you like some gin?
LISE	Um, do you have any vermouth?
MICHAEL	Oh. Uhh…
LISE	Ah.

She leaves.

MICHAEL	Okay.

MICHAEL goes into the bathroom and comes back with a bottle of pills. He shakes two out and swallows them dry, watching the TV.

Blackout.

SCENE SEVEN

The ballroom. MICHAEL and COLIN.

MICHAEL	Can you just remind me what it is we're pretending to do today?
COLIN	What's the point?
MICHAEL	No, I'm sorry, I'll follow the notes.

COLIN hands him a file, MICHAEL reads.

COLIN	So. How's it going?
MICHAEL	Uh, fine.

COLIN   Great. That's great.

MICHAEL   How's what going.

COLIN   Yeah. Right.

MICHAEL   What. Okay. Forget it.

COLIN   You bet.

> *A pause.*

You know what we all wonder, though?

MICHAEL   I do not.

COLIN   She call you "Michel?"

MICHAEL   Okay. Shut up.

COLIN   And, does that throw you?

MICHAEL   Shut up.

COLIN   I mean, there you are, right? At it. Rugging along, at your most masculine, when she comes out with "Oh, oh, tabarnac, Oh, MICHEL!"

MICHAEL   What is this, Junior high? Shut up.

COLIN   Yeah. Okay.

> *A pause.*

Lemme ask you this, then.

MICHAEL   Oh, Jesus.

COLIN   No, really. Is there some sort of strategic component to this? Are you, I don't know, trying to infiltrate their, their, their, stuff or something?

MICHAEL   No, I'm not.

COLIN   Because I could understand, if you were trying to do something, here, I'd respect that.

MICHAEL   I'm not.

COLIN   Taking one for the team. That I could understand.

MICHAEL   I don't know what I'm doing, okay? I have no plan here. And you are grossly overestimating the progress I've made.

COLIN   Sorry to hear that. Okay. It's just a thing.

MICHAEL   No, it's not even that. I can't even get her onto the friggin' couch.

COLIN   Okay, I understand. There's no point to it. Okay.

> *MATHIEU enters.*

But why the slutty behaviour all the sudden? I mean, her I get, she used to be a journalist for God's sake. But you? I mean, why.

MICHAEL   I don't know. Mathieu. Good morning.

MATHIEU   Good morning.

COLIN   What about the wife. Huh? Huh?

MICHAEL   I just, it seems like an appropriate use of my time, given the circumstances, okay? Now fuck off.

COLIN   The hell's that mean.

MATHIEU   It means he's bored, and she's antsy.

MICHAEL   Oh, my God.

COLIN   That's it?

MATHIEU   I believe so. There is also the possibility that he's trying to avoid the reality of his country's situation.

COLIN	Ahah.
MICHAEL	I'm not avoiding – can we just, stick to the agenda here?
MATHIEU	Meanwhile, she has promised to eat him alive.
COLIN	Ho ho.
MICHAEL	She – what? No. Never mind. Let's just, there's nothing happening, okay, there's no thing.
COLIN	No, sure.
MATHIEU	By all means.

>   *Silence. The men busy themselves, and LISE enters.*
>   *Activity stops. COLIN and MATHIEU can't help*
>   *looking at her. She notices, and gives MICHAEL*
>   *a look. He shrugs violently. They take their places.*

MICHAEL	Uh, okay. Good morning. Shall we begin?
MATHIEU	Yes, certainly.
MICHAEL	Right. What are we–?
COLIN	Right in front of you. Michel.
MICHAEL	All RIGHT. OKAY.
COLIN	What.
MICHAEL	You know, if something were actually going on, I'd happily put up with all of this.
MATHIEU	You mean nothing's going on?
MICHAEL	Well, not, no. No. There isn't, actually.
MATHIEU	*(to LISE)* Really?
LISE	What are we talking about?

MICHAEL	NOTHING.
MATHIEU	You guys.
LISE	What, him and me?
MATHIEU	Yes.
LISE	He's right.
MATHIEU	I thought he was just attempting to be discreet. That's a shame.
LISE	You think so? Really?
MATHIEU	Well, sure, I guess.
LISE	I don't know…
MATHIEU	One would have to admit, he's not without a crude sort of charm.
LISE	You think?
COLIN	Why not?
MICHAEL	Why not what.
COLIN	Why isn't something happening? Having trouble closing?
MICHAEL	I don't–. You know what? Ask her.
COLIN	I'm asking you, big guy.
MICHAEL	I just, I don't, can we get back to whatever the fuck is going on. Here. Today.
COLIN	Sure. You bet.
MICHAEL	Good. Okay. Thank you. *(opens the file)* Right. Uh, Let's see. Ungava. Okay. Let's talk– *(to LISE)* You are at some point going to have to address your fear. *(back to MATHIEU)* Apparently we are saying

that the Ungava territory given to you by the
government of Canada must revert...

Blackout.

SCENE EIGHT

> *MICHAEL's hotel room. LISE is on the couch.*
> *MICHAEL is shaking a martini.*

MICHAEL   ...Would you like an olive, a pickled onion, or a
twist of lemon with that?

LISE   An olive.

MICHAEL   Okay. Would you like a stuffed olive, a pitted but
unstuffed olive, or an olive with the pit still in it?

LISE   Pitted but unstuffed.

MICHAEL   Alrighty.

> *He strains the drink into a glass, and works the*
> *olive onto a frilled toothpick. He brings her the*
> *drink.*

LISE   Thank you very much.

MICHAEL   Yes. Hello.

LISE   Hello.

MICHAEL   Hi. You came back.

LISE   Yes, but–

MICHAEL   Believe me, I haven't made any assumptions about
it. Believe me. But, I'm glad.

> *A pause.*

You're fantastic.

LISE   Yes.

MICHAEL   Yes?

LISE   I mean I, uh, I, yes. Thank you very much.

> *A pause.*

Listen, Mr. Fraser, we–

MICHAEL   Ha ha. That's funny.

LISE   What.

MICHAEL   We're about to have sex. Call me Michael.

LISE   I thought you said you weren't making any assumptions.

MICHAEL   I was probably lying. Well, I was probably saying the thing that needed to be said at that moment.

LISE   I see.

MICHAEL   So, not actually lying. Yes? You were saying?

LISE   Well who the hell knows now.

MICHAEL   Sorry.

> *A fraught pause, during which they do not kiss.*

LISE   Well.

MICHAEL   Dammit. I probably should have kissed you, just then.

LISE   No, I, no. Listen. Do you find this funny?

MICHAEL   Um…

LISE   Now that we're here, and it seems, uh, imminent?

MICHAEL	Maybe. I'm trying very hard not to use that part of my brain at the moment.
LISE	I'm sorry.
MICHAEL	You don't have to be sorry.
LISE	I do. I've given you a lot of very mixed signals. Listen. I'm not normally like this. Ordinarily, I would have ignored your very gracious offer. You're just a victim of my–
MICHAEL	Of your ebullience.
LISE	Yes.
MICHAEL	Which has led to ambivalence.
LISE	Yes. Sorry. I would have stopped this sooner, but you can be very persuasive downstairs.
MICHAEL	And less so elsewhere, apparently.
LISE	No, it's me, really.
MICHAEL	Oh, well.
LISE	So, sorry. But I just don't think... I don't think...
MICHAEL	No, okay.

A pause. He looks away, she stares at him.

LISE	And now that that's settled, I want to again. God.
MICHAEL	Ha ha.
LISE	But.
MICHAEL	Yes.

A pause.

LISE	Well. I think it would have been fun.

MICHAEL   Me too.

                   A pause.

LISE   Tomorrow you go.

MICHAEL   Yes, tomorrow we walk out over… some fucking
                   thing or other.

                   She rises.

LISE   Well. Thank you for the drink.

MICHAEL   Not at all.

                   *He leads her out. The is a moment at the door where
                   she just might kiss him goodbye, then thinks better
                   of it. She goes. He watches her walk down the
                   hallway.*

MICHAEL   And listen. Congratulations, the whole
                   independence thing.

                   *He shuts the door. He turns on the TV. Still
                   standing, he notices her untouched drink. He
                   picks it up, and carefully pours the drink on the
                   carpet, grinding the olive in with his heel. He
                   leaves. He returns pantless, and, shaking tablets
                   from a bottle, settles into the couch and swallows
                   two pills dry.*

                   Blackout.

SCENE NINE

                   The ballroom. All present save MICHAEL.

COLIN   Well. I just want to say, this has been a real
                   pleasure.

                   MATHIEU smiles.

COLIN   I think we've done a real job here, in terms of optics, in terms of creating a little stability during a period of, of national instability.

MATHIEU   International. Yes.

COLIN   So, I just want to say that this has been a real pleasure, and, well done.

MATHIEU   Yes.

A pause.

COLIN   You know, we have a custom, when somebody says something nice. It's called return the fucking compliment.

MATHIEU   Yes. So do we.

Another pause. Eventually, MICHAEL bursts in the door.

MICHAEL   *Hello everyone, sorry I'm, uh, late.*

COLIN   Thank God. Let's get this over with.

MICHAEL   *I'm on the other side of the river. I'm in my office.*

COLIN   What?

MICHAEL   *I am learning, was learning the, uh, thing, the thing that copies things.*

He rolls up his sleeve, revealing a huge ink stain on his arm

COLIN   Good God. What the hell's that.

MICHAEL   *It's okay, Colin, it's okay, it's simply, uh, uh,* toner.

COLIN   It's what? What are you–

MICHAEL   *It's okay, Colin, please close the mouth. (He has memorized the next bit, and so speaks phonetically.)*

> *Good morning. I have here today's leak regarding the*
> *land of the federal within your borders. I made up this*
> *leak and have given it to the press, today's leak. (He*
> *passes paper to all.) As you can see, I've–*

COLIN   Fuck is this?

MICHAEL   *It's the leak of today.*

COLIN   Will you shut up? Talk to me.

MICHAEL   *It's, I make some changes to–*

COLIN   Federal lands issue – though contentious, not
insurmountable?? Resolution Imminent?? Parties to
continue discussions?? What the fuck is this?

MICHAEL   *It's the leak of today.*

COLIN   Fucking shut up. You gave them this?

MICHAEL   *Certainly I do, certainly.*

MATHIEU   I don't understand.

MICHAEL   *I change, I have changed my mind. This is a, what would*
you call it, a gesture.

MATHIEU   *Do you have the authority to do this?*

MICHAEL   *Sorry? Slower.*

MATHIEU   *Do you have the authority to do this?*

MICHAEL   *No. Well, yes, in a sort of way. I am in charge. Of this*
proceeding. In charge for the side of us.

MATHIEU   Yes, but–

MICHAEL   *I decide to prolong things.*

COLIN   You've decided to, what? Hey?

MICHAEL   *Prolong. I've just decided I don't want to stop this, yet.*
                Even if it doesn't really, uh, count.

COLIN   What the FUCK IS GOING ON?

MICHAEL   *(to COLIN, slowly) We are staying here. We don't stop*
                today.

COLIN   FUCKIN' SPEAK ENGLISH.

MICHAEL   *No, thanks.*

COLIN   Don't waste my time. I'm supposed to go back to
                Regina today.

MATHIEU   *Excuse me.*

COLIN   Natalie and I have a thing tomorrow night. She'll
                fuckin' kill me.

MATHIEU   *Excuse me.*

COLIN   Besides, another day of this horseshit and I'll kill
                myself.

MICHAEL   *Yes, Mathieu?*

MATHIEU   I say okay.

MICHAEL   *Really?*

MATHIEU   Yes. If you want to, we may as well.

MICHAEL   *Really?*

MATHIEU   *I don't mind, one way or the other. (to LISE) Is this what*
                you want?

LISE   *I. Well. I guess so.*

MICHAEL   *I would like that more if you could give it a little bit of*
                enthusiasm.

LISE   *Yes. All right. Yes.*

MICHAEL   *And, do you believe you can, uh, suspend the not helpful part of the brain?*

LISE   *I will try.*

MICHAEL   *Good. Excellent. (to COLIN)* They say okay. Sit down.

COLIN   Fuck that. If you think I'm gonna sit here for – I'm gonna make a phone call–

MICHAEL   I faxed the Prime Minister a copy of the leak. He knows.

COLIN   Does he approve?

MICHAEL   Like he cares. He just wants to stay out of it.

COLIN   Fucking see about that.

              COLIN glares at him, storms out. MICHAEL is looking at LISE. She rises from the table. She crosses to him, stands very close to him.

MICHAEL   Mr. Lapointe? Can we reconvene at, say, one o'clock?

LISE   Two o'clock.

MICHAEL   Mr. Lapointe? Can we reconvene at, say, two o'clock?

MATHIEU   Um, sure. All right.

LISE   And will you excuse us?

MICHAEL   And will you excuse us?

MATHIEU   No, I'd be thrilled to leave the room at this point.

              He leaves.

LISE   Hey. That was a gesture.

MICHAEL   Uh huh.

LISE   I just, I want you to know–

MICHAEL   No no. Shhhh. The walls.

> *MICHAEL takes a half-step toward LISE, who leans back onto the table, just a bit. The Tragically Hip's "Scared" begins, low. A moment like this, then the lights fade and the music comes up.*
>
> *Blackout.*

SCENE TEN

> *The ballroom, COLIN enters. He unpacks from his bulging briefcase several newspapers, some crossword anthologies, a cell phone and a two-litre bottle of Diet Coke. Meanwhile, LISE enters. Seeing COLIN, she attempts to busy herself on the other side of the room.*

COLIN   So. You're his personality.

LISE   I beg your pardon?

COLIN   In the campaign. You were Lapointe's personality. He'd say something, then you'd come out and repeat what he said, but warmly. It was very effective. Whose idea was that?

LISE   Oh. Well, our style just sort of naturally evolved, based on our particular–

COLIN   Okay, so don't tell me. It was great. We couldn't compete with that. Obviously. Maybe if we had someone like you on our side, we could have. But we didn't.

LISE   No.

COLIN   No. We sure didn't. So. What do you get to be? In the new republic.

LISE   Same job, more or less.

COLIN   Imagine you'd have your pick of things.

LISE   Yes. Well. I guess I do. But I like Intergovernmental Affairs.

COLIN   Yes you do.

                A beat.

LISE   Ha ha.

COLIN   Fuck. I promised myself I wasn't going to use that joke.

                A pause.

                Lisa. Lise, sorry. Ms Fréchette. I… sorry. Listen. About him. I know what this is, okay? Well, not really, I mean I have no actual experience with this sort of thing. To tell you the truth, you people are sort of a mystery to me. Women. I married my wife a long time ago, and it came as an immense relief, let me tell you. This isn't about me.

                And I don't imagine there's anything I could tell you you don't already know. But I'm gonna anyway, the privilege of advanced years. Uh, he's a great guy. And I kind of admire him for pulling that stunt, don't tell him I said so. He made an awful lot of people jump by prolonging this. Finally learning to take control a bit, run the room. But he's a politician. A man of successive sincerities. And the qualities we're cultivating in him are not necessarily the ones somebody like you might be looking for in a fella. If you asked him, I'm sure he could tell you what he wants, but I'm not sure he'd give you the same answer twice in a row. I mean, I know he doesn't come off as particularly dangerous, but maybe it'd be in your interest to consider him so.

LISE   Thank you.

COLIN	By which of course you mean "shut up."
LISE	Not at all. I appreciate your candour.
COLIN	Well. Anyway.

The Quebec door opens, and MATHIEU comes in.

MATHIEU	Lise. Colin.
LISE	Good morning.
COLIN	*(sitting and erecting a newspaper)* Uh huh.

MICHAEL comes in.

MICHAEL	Good morning.
LISE & MATHIEU	Good morning.
MICHAEL	*(to LISE)* Good morning.
LISE	Yes.
MICHAEL	I'll say. Colin.
COLIN	What.
MICHAEL	Morning.
COLIN	Absolutely.
MICHAEL	Okay. I think we should have a light morning, followed by lunch.
MATHIEU	All right.
COLIN	Smashing.
MICHAEL	Now. Does anyone have anything they want to say? To get things going today? Colin?
COLIN	*(still behind the paper)* Sorry?

MICHAEL	Anything you want to start with, today?
COLIN	No. Yes. Is "guerrilla rebel" redundant?
MICHAEL	Thank you, Colin. Anyone else?
	A pause, then:
LISE	Well, seeing as how we're just talking, we could revisit the debt.
MICHAEL	Debt, sure, fantastic. Your dirty little secret.
LISE	*(to MATHIEU) Okay with you?*
MATHIEU	*Why not? It was hilarious last time.*
LISE	Well, I had a thought. We would agree to leave with as large a debt as we came in with. You know, proportionally figured in today's dollars. The same debt we had when we entered into the Act of Union.
MICHAEL	Well, that sounds reasonable. Do you have a number?
LISE	Well yes, but I think you should figure that out for yourself, and we'll see if we match up.
MICHAEL	Yes.
LISE	Not to be coy.
MICHAEL	No no. Colin?
COLIN	Just a sec. Yes?
MICHAEL	Go and get that figure, would you?
COLIN	Geez, I'm real busy here…
MICHAEL	Off you go.

COLIN *sighs, puts down the paper, stands, sighs, and leaves.*

MATHIEU   Shall we talk about the underlying principles involved here? In that kind of a split?

MICHAEL   Why?

MATHIEU   No reason. I thought it might be fun.

MICHAEL   Well, sure. Okay. But first: how'd everybody sleep?

MATHIEU   Very well, thank you.

LISE   *(simultaneous)* Yes, thanks.

MICHAEL   What kind of underwear is everyone wearing today?

MATHIEU   Um.

MICHAEL   Anybody as sore as I am this morning?

MATHIEU   Um. Ha ha. Okay. If you'll excuse me, I'm just going… leave the room.

He goes. LISE stands, walks to the geographic centre of the table, overturns a tumbler and pours herself some water. She leans into the table very slightly to do this. She drinks, also for his benefit. She sits.

MICHAEL   Thanks.

LISE   Uh huh.

They are staring at each other.

Michael. What do you want?

MICHAEL   That's right.

They continue to stare. COLIN comes in.

COLIN   Yes, ha ha, very funny.

LISE   Yes?

COLIN   Yes. Very funny. *(He goes back to his paper.)*

MICHAEL   What.

COLIN   *(from behind the paper)* Quebec had no debt when it entered into the Act of Union. Ontario had a big one, Quebec had nothing.

MICHAEL   Really?

COLIN   Yeah. Hilarious, what?

MICHAEL   Well. We'll have to examine that. *(to LISE)* Lunch?

LISE   Sure.

MICHAEL   *(rising)* That's lunch, Colin.

COLIN   *(doesn't move)* Uh huh.

> *MICHAEL makes several vague gestures to LISE. She nods. They leave through their respective doors. The Quebec door opens, and MATHIEU enters, after making sure the coast is clear.*

MATHIEU   Um, Colin?

COLIN   That's lunch, big guy.

MATHIEU   Ah.

> *At a loss, MATHIEU sits.*

COLIN   Aren't you hungry?

MATHIEU   Well, it's ten fifteen. Maybe later. Could I... look at a section of that?

COLIN   Sure.

> *As COLIN hands him the front section of* The Globe and Mail:

Hey. What are you doing here?

MATHIEU   What do you mean?

COLIN   Well, we aren't doing anything.

MATHIEU   Yes. I know. Nice, isn't it?

COLIN   Don't you have a country to run?

MATHIEU   *(sitting, erecting the paper)* Ah. Well. I am on it, as they say. Big guy.

> *COLIN regards MATHIEU, then goes back to his paper.*
>
> *Blackout.*

Scene Eleven

> *MICHAEL's hotel room. A nature program on the TV. There's a knock at the door. He opens it.*

COLIN   Hi. You got any scotch?

MICHAEL   Um, sure. C'mon in.

> *They walk in. MICHAEL finds the bottle and hands it over.*

COLIN   No. I meant, let's have a drink.

MICHAEL   Oh.

> *He pours. They sit.*

MICHAEL   Everything all right?

COLIN   Huh? Yeah. Why.

MICHAEL   Well, it's just, I don't know, you're... here.

COLIN   Relax. I just don't feel like sitting in the room.

MICHAEL   No, sure.

COLIN   I'm finding our talks are not leaving me spent by day's end. I wind up thinking. *(indicates the* TV*)* Do you mind?

> *MICHAEL turns off the* TV. *Silence.*

You ever meet Trudeau?

MICHAEL   Once. I was a teenager.

COLIN   Huh.

> *A pause.*

MICHAEL   You knew him.

COLIN   Huh? Yeah. Fuckin' guy. Ten minutes with him and you walked out convinced there was actually a fuckin' point.

> *A pause.*

Well. At least he's not around to see this almighty bullshit.

> *A pause.*

You know what I did before this?

MICHAEL   Nothing. You've always done this.

COLIN   Nope. I sold insurance for two years before my first campaign. My territory was called North. Just North. Which meant everything that wasn't Regina, basically. So I met a lot of people. And do you know what they all had in common?

MICHAEL   Nobody needed insurance?

COLIN   You know what else they had in common?

MICHAEL   No.

COLIN   They all knew they were getting fucked. By the government. By something called the government. And not only that, but who cares about the rest of the country, because these people are the only ones anywhere getting fucked. I mean, that's the attitude of all these people, every single person outside of Regina. Expressed with a belief, with a certainty you see evidence of nowhere else in their lives.

So eventually, I quit that, I get married, a guy comes to me, blah blah blah, I ran in my first campaign, me and Natalie, and during the course of that, I realized: that's the attitude of everyone IN Regina, too. They're getting fucked, and everyone else isn't. Not open hostility toward anyone, the whole rest of the country just sort of doesn't count on account of they're not the ones getting it from "the government." And, now, of course, I've been all over now, 37 years, and that's what everyone everywhere believes. The only thing we believe in as a group is our individual, separate fuckings courtesy of the government.

I always thought I'd like to spend a year, target some place, and just spend a year really fucking that place. Really, actively giving it to the people somewhere. Then, when they see what that's actually like, to be the focus of our displeasure, they'll shut up, and then we move on. And we fuck the bejesus out of somewhere else. Like I don't know, put all of the nation's garbage there, and wreck the phones and put the loudest fuckin NATO launchpad right downtown. And it's my dream that when we're in the middle of doing all that, the people from the first place go: "Hey. Cut it out. You tried that with us, too. Don't do it to them." Then we go all across the country like that, until everybody knows what a good fucking really feels like, and everyone gives a shit about the fucking their neighbour got.

There's a knock at the door. MICHAEL rises.

Nice, eh? My dream consists of getting 30 million people to shut the fuck up.

MICHAEL opens the door. It's LISE.

MICHAEL   Oh! Hi.

LISE   Hello Michel. I have a little sur–

MICHAEL   Colin's here. C'mon in.

LISE   Oh. Should I...?

MICHAEL   C'mon in.

> *MICHAEL and LISE enter. LISE is wearing a trenchcoat.*

COLIN   Oh, hey. Hi. I should...

LISE   No, please. Sit.

MICHAEL   No no. Finish your drink.

COLIN   Alrighty.

> *He sits. MICHAEL fixes a drink for LISE.*

MICHAEL   Colin was just telling me about his first campaign.

LISE   Ah.

COLIN   Yeah. Riveting. How are you tonight?

LISE   Fine, thank you.

COLIN   Take off your coat.

LISE   Um, no thank you. I think I'll just keep it on for now.

COLIN   Aren't you roasting?

MICHAEL   Let me take your coat.

LISE   (*giggling*) No, thank you. I'd better keep it on.

COLIN   Huh? Oh, Jesus. What a fucking asshole. I'd better go.

Rises, downs his scotch.

MICHAEL   Colin. Really. You don't have to go.

COLIN   No. I don't want to get in the way of your thing here. Ms Fréchette.

LISE   Mr. Patterson.

COLIN   Have a nice evening. I envy you both the way you've found for dealing with, uh, things.

COLIN leaves.

LISE   This is hard for him.

MICHAEL   It seems so.

A pause.

Hello.

LISE   Hello. I have a little surprise.

MICHAEL   I, yes, so I see.

LISE   I also have a small proposal.

MICHAEL   Great.

There's a knock at the door. MICHAEL goes. It's MATHIEU.

Monsieur Lapointe.

MATHIEU   Mr. Fraser. I hope I'm not disturbing you.

MICHAEL	Well–
MATHIEU	*(entering)* I've just been thinking about what you were saying this afternoon.
MICHAEL	Really?
MATHIEU	Yes. I found it—hello, Lise—I found it most interesting.
MICHAEL	What, um, what exactly did I say this afternoon?
MATHIEU	About the constitution.
MICHAEL	Uh huh.
MATHIEU	Yes.
MICHAEL	What exactly did I say about the constitution?
MATHIEU	Well, you implied that repatriating it might have been a mistake on your part.
MICHAEL	I did? Oh, well. I was probably just being polite.
MATHIEU	Nonetheless. Oh. I'm not interrupting anything here, am I?

A pause.

MICHAEL	Um, I suppose not.
MATHIEU	Great. I found I was enjoying our talk, and I was saddened by its premature conclusion. Now. Repatriation.
MICHAEL	Yes. As I said, in hindsight, it was probably a bad idea to leave you out.
MATHIEU	Yes, that's just it. I disagree.
MICHAEL	You do.
MATHIEU	Absolutely. Repatriation got us where we are today.

MICHAEL   Yes, I see.

MATHIEU   I wish you'd repatriate something weekly. Ha ha.

MICHAEL   I see. Well, in that case, I take it back.

MATHIEU   You what?

MICHAEL   I take back what I said about it being a mistake.

MATHIEU   But, you can't.

MICHAEL   I can't?

MATHIEU   No. This isn't a schoolyard. You can't take it back. You can refute it, contradict yourself, deny you said it at all, but you can't take it back.

MICHAEL   I see.

MATHIEU   That's the thing about being a grown-up.

MICHAEL   Uh huh.

LISE   You guys gonna be long?

MICHAEL   No we are not. Mathieu. Can I call you Mathieu?

MATHIEU   Certainly.

MICHAEL   I don't mean to be critical, and please don't take this the wrong way, but this proceeding could stand a little less of your attitude.

MATHIEU   My attitude.

MICHAEL   Yes. This whole thing is sort of getting poisoned, I think, by the fact that you seem to know exactly what you're doing.

MATHIEU   Really.

MICHAEL   So, please, cut it out, this, this… whole thing. Because it's your least attractive feature.

MATHIEU   Very well.

MICHAEL   No, see? You're still doing it.

MATHIEU   Yes. Sorry. I do apologize. Very foolish of me.

MICHAEL   Sorry to be so blunt.

MATHIEU   No, no. It's true. It's something I've been accused of my whole life. Thank you.

MICHAEL   Um, sure. We can continue this tomorrow, if you like.

MATHIEU   Good. Yes. All right. I'd love to know how you really feel about the constitution.

MICHAEL   Sure. Uh, I'll have to bone up.

MATHIEU   Good. And I apologize for my attitude.

MICHAEL   Not at all.

       MATHIEU leaves.

       That poor man.

LISE   Oh, please.

MICHAEL   No, no. He seems, I don't know, lonely somehow.

LISE   He's the happiest guy in the country. In both.

MICHAEL   I guess.

LISE   Hey. C'mere.

       They kiss.

MICHAEL   You're fantastic.

LISE   Uh, yeah.

       She moves away.

Listen, would you mind not saying that?

MICHAEL   What. That you're fantastic? Does it have some
            connotation for you people I don't know about?

LISE   No, it's just… I'd prefer it if we keep this on this
            level. You know?

MICHAEL   The level that doesn't include compliments?

LISE   Just, the physical, okay? I want this to remain…

MICHAEL   Fun. Okay.

LISE   Okay.

MICHAEL   But I can't take any responsibility for what comes
            out of my mouth in the heat of passion. I'm likely
            to loudly declare your adequacy.

LISE   That's fine.

            She leads him to the bedroom.

MICHAEL   Oh, Lise, oh, God, Lise, you're so, so, competent! So
            ergonomic! Oh, God, Lise, I find you to be within
            expected parameters!

LISE   Shut up.

MICHAEL   Yes! Lise! Yes! In all probability, yes! Plus or minus
            two percentage points nine times out of ten, YES!

            Blackout.

Scene Twelve

            *Lights snap up in the negotiating room. Everyone
            in their places.*

MICHAEL   Yes. The answer is yes. Repatriation was a mistake.
            But you know what?

MATHIEU   What?

MICHAEL   It was your mistake.

MATHIEU   Our mistake?

MICHAEL   Yes. In '79, Trudeau was gone. He retired. There was another election, and they begged Trudeau to come back. He did. He won. And he said "Okay, as long as I'm here, I might as well repatriate the constitution." You know, posterity, and whatnot. But you put him there. He got 68% of the Quebec vote, and won 74 out of Quebec's 75 seats. Nice blouse. So tell me, why would you do that? The guy spends most of his career dismissing the notion of sovereignty, dismissing it as the misguided, childish mewling of a bunch of people labouring under a victim's view of history, dismissing you as only he can, and after you're finally rid of him, you decide you can't live without him. I mean, what the hell was that?

MATHIEU   Yes.

MICHAEL   Yes?

MATHIEU   I can see why you might be tempted to make that argument. It's a funny one.

COLIN   *(popping open a can of nuts)* Um, excuse me. Fuck are we doing today?

MICHAEL   Mathieu wanted to continue our discussion about their primary grievance.

COLIN   Oh. Swell.

MATHIEU   I would not describe the constitution as our "primary grievance." And as for your assertion that this is a predicament of our own making, I'm afraid that we as a people have never managed to act with the kind of homogeneous political will that you endow us with. I wish my people could take the credit for things getting to this point. But the fact is, we're here thanks to your stupidity. English Canada's stupidity.

MICHAEL Whoa! Hey now.

COLIN *(simultaneously)* Aw, fuck. Here we go.

MATHIEU It's true. Tell me. The BNA Act. Is it a compact between two founding nations, or is it a blueprint for the confederation of several disparate regions?

COLIN The fuck cares?

MATHIEU Yes, that's true, Colin. I'll give you that. But the fact is, we've been walking around, you and us, thinking it was two different things. Even if we didn't care, Colin. Your behaviour based on one assumption, ours based on another.

The lights begin to fade.

MICHAEL No no, I've heard this one before. You're going to say that for hundreds of years you've thought that the agreement was just for you and me, for us, and that when everyone else started showing up, bringing their interests to the table you guys got pushed–

MATHIEU No no, that's not it–

MICHAEL Sure it is. You want to pretend that a treaty between our founding nations got diluted every time a new province...

Blackout. After a moment in the dark, the lights come back up. Ties are loosened, people have moved about.

MICHAEL ...But that's not the point.

LISE Of course it's the point. That's the whole point. That's always been the point, in a way. It has nothing to do with who struck what deal with whom, or whether or not anybody seemed content for a number of years when actually they weren't. The point is, we didn't begin properly. We didn't begin on proper terms. You can't have a negotiation between two groups if one is utterly powerless.

COLIN   Sure you can. Those are the most fun.

LISE   No, you can't.

MICHAEL   You know, the focus of your rage should be the mother country. France screwed you long before we got there. France is to blame. Hate the French, not us.

COLIN   Go ahead. It's easy. Most of the world already does.

LISE   *(to MICHAEL)* What do you mean?

MATHIEU   He's alluding to the fact that France allowed 10,000 people to come, then no more.

MICHAEL   That's right. Apparently, they kept you from building a proper colony. They thought the whole idea of starting up another one was just an immense pain in the ass.

COLIN   Fucking France. De Gaulle shows up right at the height of the shit. Right when things were at their most volatile, he decides to pitch his two cents in. But while he was standing up there saying "Vive La free Quebec," DeGaulle was throwing Bretons and Corsicans and Basques in jail for wanting exactly the same thing for themselves. That's fucking France for you. That's your closest ally, you realize that.

MATHIEU   It will always be where we came from, but France is our ally, not our moral compass. But let me ask you something.

MICHAEL   What.

COLIN   *(simultaneously)* What.

MATHIEU	No no, Michael.
COLIN	Why are you looking at me if you're talking to him?
MATHIEU	I'm not. I... oh. I apologize. It's this eye. My left one is a straying eye. Is that what you call it?
COLIN	A wandering eye?
MICHAEL	A lazy eye?
MATHIEU	Yes, exactly. I'm sorry.
COLIN	It's okay.
MICHAEL	Please, I'm sorry. I didn't know.
MATHIEU	Not at all. Michael. Let me ask you a question.
MICHAEL	All right.
MATHIEU	Are you in love with Ms Fréchette?
LISE	*Mathieu? Excuse me, but...*
MICHAEL	Sorry, what?
MATHIEU	Are you in love with Ms Fréchette?
MICHAEL	I, uhh. I don't see where you're going with this, Mathieu.
MATHIEU	Answer the question, and I'll show you where I'm going.
MICHAEL	I mean, what possible relevance to the subject can our relationship, if in fact we are having one, which I strenuously–
MATHIEU	Okay, okay. Let me ask you this, then: Do you understand the distinction between loving something and being in love with something? Or someone?

MICHAEL   Uhh…

MATHIEU   Can you see the distinction between having an affinity for something, and having an appetite for it?

Lights start to fade.

MICHAEL   Well, sure, I think. Sure. I think. But maybe you'd explain it?

MATHIEU   Well, it seems to me, that when one comes up against something one likes, one has the choice between consuming it and being intimate with it. And I think this conversation about our relationship would get somewhere faster if we admit that we're a bunch of consumers.

MICHAEL   Which is a bad thing?

MATHIEU   The compulsive need to eat something instead of sitting beside it? Yes, I think it is.

COLIN   You talking about me?

MATHIEU   No, I think we all have the same problem.

COLIN   But you were looking at – oh. Shit. Sorry…

Blackout. More time passes. More dishevelment, more movement. Lights up. MICHAEL and MATHIEU are seated, spent, LISE and COLIN are on their feet.

…It's a real skill. You have to know rope. And then, you know, if it is a chicken, at that point you can hang it upside down and slit its throat. It's important that you don't upset the chicken, as much as possible, so the tying up and the slitting must be done with an air of efficiency and even casualness. A chicken that's upset when killed tastes differ… *(everyone's looking at him)* What.

LISE   No, I said "trust." Do you know what it is to "trust."

COLIN   Oh, do you know what it is to TRUST. I see. Sorry. I been married thirty-seven years, I think I know a thing or two about trust.

LISE   Our problem is, we will never, ever trust you.

COLIN   Oh, shit, well, who trusts who, really. I mean really. Trust comes and goes, you can't trust it. You only have a real relationship when you figure out how to genuinely take the other party for granted. Which is harder than it sounds.

MICHAEL   Yes, that's... hoo-eee...

LISE   What?

MICHAEL   We did. We, when we started, you and I, we withheld it. There was no trust implied in our, um.... No, what it was, is, we didn't need, as a precondition of... we didn't.... No. Sorry. Never mind. Carry on.

LISE   We don't like the rules. We don't like the game. We will not play.

MICHAEL   No no, the game is not, we don't have to be playing... *(He rises.)* Look. For four hundred years we have had a thing. Okay, maybe we both thought a little sloppily about what that thing was, but, it was a thing. We had. And we had it among us. And it made us. And we made it. Do you like to dance?

MATHIEU   Michael, are you...?

MICHAEL   Fine? Are you fine? I believe so sincerely. Do you like to dance?

LISE   At the right occasion, yes.

MICHAEL   I loved it. I don't do it anymore, much. In cabinet, we don't get a lot of dance functions. Friggin' ambassadors, they get all the dance functions.

COLIN   Michael?

MICHAEL   I'm moving across the floor, all the girls are standing over there and among them, deep among them is Jenny Norfolk, and I know, we both know what it is I'm coming to ask. She sees me, she's not looking, but she sees me, and over I come, like I'm going over the side, onto the beach, into the breech, the, yes, breech is her. The breech is her. And we… uh, oh fuck. What was I.

COLIN   You okay?

MICHAEL   *(sits)* I'm. I'm simply.

COLIN   Let's go eat something.

MICHAEL   No! I'm just, I have a deficit. I have a disorder. My attention. Is a, is in debt, a deficit disorder. I take stuff for it. I take this shit I've taken for like thirty years. I'm a couple of hours late for them. I need. Here. *(takes out his room key, whizzes it across the table to COLIN)* Go and get me my Ritalin. And I'll just shut the fuck up until you get back.

COLIN   Okay.

MICHAEL   You know, bring the bottle.

COLIN   Okay. Take it easy until I get back.

> *He goes. A silence. LISE pours some water and gives it to MICHAEL. When she gives it to him, he pulls her down and whispers in her ear. We can't hear him, but the surtitle reads: "On ne danse plus. Viens me voir ce soir, on dansera."*

LISE   *(rises)* Okay.

> *There is more silence. LISE sits.*

MICHAEL   You're fantastic.

> *A pause.*

Sorry. Forget I said that. Nothing's, you know, happening. It's just a thing.

A pause.

Here's the thing I must tell you quickly before he returns.

MATHIEU   Michael. Let's just wait–

MICHAEL   No no. Listen. You'll never have this opportunity again. You have to know what we are. Why we... listen.

> *MICHAEL exerts an enormous amount of energy to focus long enough to get the following out.*

I had an idea, as a child, I don't know where from, but the thing is, nothing since then has come along to replace the idea, or to disprove it. The idea is, I've always thought, no matter how good I get at being a person, a person who lives among people, an apparently kind, considerate person, a worthy person; a person who will someday run this country; no matter how many layers of decency and respectfulness and whatnot I apply to my person, that a moment will come, will come for us all, when my true self will be revealed. It will happen one day, in public, like: I'll be walking somewhere, feeling smug or happy, or competent, and I'll step off a curb and there it will be: a baby or something in the roadway, and the bus speeding down on it, and I have no time to do anything other than get the baby or not. Act or not act. In a reflexive fashion, a fashion that reflects what I truly am, totally regardless of how I've lived up to that second. Mathieu, Lise: I've spent my entire life avoiding that moment. My whole adult life has been an attempt to see that moment coming in time to not have it happen. To keep that moment, and what you might find out about me in it, from coming. And I don't know you people, I really don't understand what you people are like, but all my people are more or less like that. I'm just, I'm very afraid that this is where I'm going to meet that moment, in this room. And I find, all I want is, let it not be me. Let it be the next guy. Let mine be some other moment, not this one, not this room, not now.

Those among us who want you to stay, who swear we can't understand why you would leave, most of us, we just don't want to be here when it happens. Which isn't the same as not wanting you to go. Don't tell Colin I said that. He'll be pissed.

MATHIEU   No. I won't.

        A pause.

MICHAEL   Did you ever have the impression that we may be the least qualified people in the country for this job?

MATHIEU   Not all the time.

MICHAEL   Me either. Not all the time.

        A pause.

        (to MATHIEU) You're a deeply sad man, aren't you.

        A pause.

        (to LISE) What are we going to do?

LISE   Just wait.

MICHAEL   No, I mean you and me. I know, I know but oh, God, I want to, I feel like I could just–

LISE   Michael. Just wait for Colin.

MICHAEL   Yeah. Where did he…?

        A pause.

MATHIEU   Okay. Let me ask you this before he comes back.

MICHAEL	Yes. Good.
MATHIEU	Do you know what motivates us?
MICHAEL	Do I...? Ha ha. Holy fuck. To us you guys are about as transparent as a crop circle.
MATHIEU	What motivates us, all of us, is fear. You and me. You described yours. But you don't recognize mine.
MICHAEL	Recognize your what?
MATHIEU	Listen. Look at me.
MICHAEL	I am. You look at me.
MATHIEU	No, look at this eye.
MICHAEL	Oh, yeah. There you are. Sorry. Okay, go.
MATHIEU	The reason we appear irrational to you is because we aren't being rational. What we want makes no sense, but it's our only choice. The only thing we fear less than staying is going. So it's fear that moves us, just like yours moves you.
MICHAEL	Hey! That's good. Okay. We can use that.
MATHIEU	No, we can't. And don't tell Colin.
MICHAEL	Okay. But, thanks. It means a lot, Mathieu.
MATHIEU	I'll deny I said it.
MICHAEL	I know. But you can't take it back.

COLIN rushes in.

COLIN	Shut up! Michael! Shut up!
MICHAEL	No problem. Where the hell were you?

COLIN hands him his Ritalin.

COLIN   Listen to this. I'd like to read a report, just handed
                 to me outside:

                 US President Frank Gifford has scrambled a large
                 airborne attack force to the air base at Plattsburgh,
                 New York and is mobilizing a light infantry
                 company from Fort Drum, New York, to take
                 up positions in northern Maine.

                 LISE gets up and goes out the Quebec door.

                 (after the retreating LISE) Yeah. Good idea. *(reading)*
                 He is expected to announce his intention to move
                 the troops into the newly sovereign Republic of
                 Quebec should the need for a stabilizing force
                 become apparent. Quote: "The US has interests in
                 Quebec, security interests and economic ones, and
                 it frankly makes us nervous that the airspace above
                 Quebec could be compromised. We also have
                 legitimate concerns about the possible interruption
                 of oil flowing from the Quebec region of Labrador."
                 Unquote. Gifford has said he's watching "with
                 great interest" the negotiations now taking place in
                 Hull between the Canadian government and that of
                 Quebec. Do you know what this means?

MICHAEL   Yes. It means the United States thinks Labrador is
                 part of Quebec.

MATHIEU   May I...?

COLIN   Yup.

                 Gives MATHIEU the piece of paper.

MATHIEU   Well. I think that, given this new, um, situation, we
                 will suspend this meeting and allow the actual
                 negotiations to proceed as quickly as they can, in
                 the interest of stabilizing Quebec's position.

MICHAEL   Uh, okay. Sure. You bet.

COLIN   Well, no, actually. We can't stop. We're it. Our
                 side just got up and walked away from the real

negotiations. The government of Canada has decided that in the light of these developments, our bargaining position has radically changed for the better. Everything that was on offer is now off the table. We're gonna start over, and since everyone's watching this room, we're gonna do it here. You and us.

MATHIEU   We are not prepared at this time to continue–

COLIN   If we stop these talks, the US will take that as a sign of complete destabilization and they'll move in on your capital.

> *LISE has re-entered the room, holding a piece of paper. She nods to MATHIEU.*

MICHAEL   Um, I missed some of that. What's going on? We have to what?

COLIN   So, grab a seat. You're not going anywhere. Until we're done with ya.

> *Blackout.*

ACT II

*The ballroom. Before house light goes down,
MICHAEL enters, carrying a piece of paper and
a butter knife. He consults the paper, and begins to
use the butter knife to scrape off a bit of wallpaper.
House light fades. Music begins: "The Completists"
by The Tragically Hip. Blackout.*

*When the lights come back up, LISE is in the room,
near the Quebec door. MICHAEL is standing on the
table, working something tiny and black out of the
chandelier with the butter knife. Music fades.*

MICHAEL   ...not that I hold that against you. Please don't
misunderstand me. I actually think that's a point
in your favour.

Okay, I'm not being clear here. My only goal in this
was to be clear, to clearly state my newfound point
of view, and I'm not even doing that. So far, I view
this meeting as a failure; I don't know how you feel
about it so far, but for me, this is a failure. So far.
So. But. I remain determined. Okay:

It's not you, it's me. Let me repeat that: not you;
me. I have been forced to reevaluate what it is
we're doing, and you haven't, at least you haven't
said you have, but, on the other hand, given the
level you've said you want this to occur on, the
level of "fun," I don't suppose you'd have told me
if you'd been engaging in any reevaluatory activity.
And let me just inject here that it's nervousness and
not some absurd pedanticism that makes me coin
things like "reevaluatory."

> *MICHAEL gets down off the table and crawls
> underneath; we hear him scraping with the
> butterknife and he reemerges every once in a
> while to put a tiny black thing on the table.*

Did I want to reevaluate? I did not. It was more
or less thrust upon me, and boy oh boy, do I ever
hate that notion. I prefer, for the most part, to be in
control of choosing what things I spend my time
doing. I mean, it's commonly known as adulthood,
for fuck's sake. Anyway, it was happening, all the
time, during all our time together, as tremendous
as it was, every minute, a nagging something
deep inside me, operating without my authority,
impeding my ability to fully engage in the, fun.

I'm sorry about this. I'm sorry about all of it.

Anyhoo, my current point of view is that what
we are engaged in is a mistake, mistake being
absolutely the wrong word, maybe even an
objectionable one because of its smallness, its
inability to convey gravity. So not a mistake, but
a mistake, if you see what I...

And I'm not a big fan of fault or of blame, but I'm
willing to accept either one of those, or both even.
Again, me, all me. Not you.

LISE   I understand.

MICHAEL   *(emerging from under the table)* No, that's, ha ha, you
don't. But as God is my witness, you, uh, will.

>*He works the upholstery off of MATHIEU's chair
>and finds another black thing.*

You see, look, it's, I– *(He freezes for a couple of
beats, then:)* I've decided to unilaterally declare
my feelings for you.

LISE   You...?

MICHAEL   That actually sounds worse than I thought it
would.

LISE   You...?

MICHAEL	Didn't think that was possible. Yes. Sorry. I'm very sorry. They are large feelings, and they simply can't be contained by the rules of our current arrangement. I can tell you exactly when they asserted themselves, these feelings, a couple of nights ago, prone, your lips an inch or two from my face, I can tell you about that time sometime, and no doubt I will.

No doubt I will. But for now, what I'm saying now, is, they, these large feelings constitute the basis for the undeniable sensation that this has been a mistake. That even as I continued to engage or appeared to engage lightly in our thing, I found that that was getting harder and harder to do. As my feelings got, well, larger and larger. Now.

I have no plan, and I think I'm being honest when I say that. I don't tell you this because I have some goal in mind, regarding you or us or even this meeting's outcome, I just thought it time to let you in on what I've been feeling. I know you don't want to know about my feelings, but, well, sorry. I found I couldn't exist within the constraints of our current arrangement any longer.

LISE	What are you saying.
MICHAEL	Yes, well, there, that's the, uh, ha ha, isn't it. What is he saying…
LISE	What is it you want.
MICHAEL	Exactly. I don't know. But I just, I at this moment feel capable of anything.

A pause.

And that's all you. And before we descend into discussions and proposals and the ugly nuts and bolts of what we might do, you and I, what the ramifications of my unilateral declaration might be, before we talk about any of it (and God knows it could be a very short talk), I want that we should just be here, in this moment, extend this moment as long as possible. This moment in which I feel expansive, and rich and fully, fully USED for the first time since I don't know when. Because, and I say this as someone who knows you like nobody, in my way: you feel like this too. We feel like this, and we feel like this separately, and I say let's feel like this together, in this moment.

A pause.

LISE   Are you out of your fucking mind?

MICHAEL   And now, the moment's gone. Well, okay then, tell me you don't feel it. Tell me you don't feel the same.

LISE walks out the Quebec door.

You see, you can't.

MICHAEL finishes with the small black things and puts them into a glass. COLIN enters.

COLIN   Michael.

MICHAEL   Colin.

COLIN   Who you talking to?

MICHAEL   Nobody. The room. How are you?

COLIN   Tremendous. Ready to go. You take your meds?

MICHAEL   Yes.

COLIN   Excellent. Did you see the paper this morning?

MICHAEL   Uhh, no.

COLIN   Disney's made an offer on PEI.

MICHAEL   Aw, for fuck's sake.

> *A pause, while MICHAEL and COLIN consider this. Then:*

MICHAEL   Is it any good?

COLIN   The cat is among the pigeons, as they say. *(handing MICHAEL a huge file)* Here's how today is going to go.

> *MICHAEL drops the file.*

MICHAEL   Thanks.

COLIN   No, look at it. Our real guys made that. There are two dozen senior bureaucrats and advisors and rich guys and consultants in there who worked very hard on this.

MICHAEL   Okay.

COLIN   This is what we're going to do to them while we've got the chance. You must do what's in there. No fucking around. Okay?

MICHAEL   Okay, okay.

COLIN   You are hereby relieved of the burden of thinking.

MICHAEL   *(He starts reading.)* Righto.

> *A pause.*

COLIN   Did you hear? More than half our troops stationed in Quebec have defected.

MICHAEL   *(still reading)* Huh. Westmount still blockaded?

COLIN   Uh huh. Mulroney's still trapped in his house.

MICHAEL   Well, that's something, I guess. *(looking up)* All right. Good. Let's go. Where are they?

COLIN   I dunno.

> *MICHAEL goes to the Quebec door, knocks on it,
> and opens it.*

MICHAEL Hellllooo? We're all set. Can we get started in here, please? Hello?

> *MATHIEU comes to the door.*

Hi. Can we–?

MATHIEU Yes.

> *MATHIEU enters. He sits. MICHAEL lingers by
> the Quebec door, but finally takes his seat.*

Morning.

COLIN Morning.

MICHAEL Morning. Well. Here we are. Kind of a different feeling in the room this morning.

MATHIEU Indeed.

COLIN Ha ha.

MICHAEL Right. Fantastic. Let's get right to it. We all know your position has been weakened considerably by the actions of our American friends.

MATHIEU That's not strictly true–

MICHAEL No no, I'm talking now. So, given your position currently, the federal side has decided to change its approach to several key areas in this negotiation. To put it simply: we will now try to fuck you. That's what this is. *(holding up the file)* We've decided to take advantage of you while we can, and this contains our strategy for doing so. It contains our opening positions on various matters, what we expect you to come back with, what we're actually willing to settle for. This is how we plan to fuck you before you go. Here. *(He gives it to MATHIEU.)* Have a look.

COLIN   Hey! What are you doing?

MICHAEL   *(to COLIN, with surprising viciousness)* Shut the fuck
            up. It was you and your kind that got us into this.
            Sit the fuck down. You're done. *(to MATHIEU)*
            I give you our strategy to show you what you
            would have been left with by the end of this
            negotiation. I give you our strategy, because
            I don't intend to use it.

            > *MICHAEL is pouring water into the glass of tiny
            > black things.*

            These are all of the listening devices planted in this
            room by our side. The room is now bug-free, as far
            as the Federal government is concerned. *(handing
            the glass to COLIN)* Can you see that CSIS gets these
            back?

            I do not expect you to remove the bugs you've
            placed in here. I don't care if you do. And I from
            this moment refuse to participate in any leaks to the
            press. If I have something to say to them, I will tell
            them. If I don't, I won't.

            I find myself unwilling to continue in our current,
            rather empty arrangement. I also find I have little
            enthusiasm for what my government wants me to
            do. So: I have no plan. I do have a goal. My goal is
            simple, and it's based on a feeling, not that I'm a
            big fan of them, but, sometimes, you know, the fuck
            can you do. Currently, in fact, I am utterly subject
            to a whole shitload, and, well, yahoo. My goal. My
            goal is: don't go.

MATHIEU   What?

MICHAEL   Don't go.

MATHIEU   But–

MICHAEL   Don't go.

COLIN   Aw fuck.

> *LISE enters.*

LISE   Hey!

MICHAEL   Lise–

LISE   Could you, come here for a second? Can I talk to you? Sort of?

MICHAEL   Of course. Excuse me, gentlemen.

> *MICHAEL rises and crosses to LISE.*

Listen, I just, I hope I haven't–

> *LISE lunges at MICHAEL, kisses him. Then, after a moment's consideration:*

LISE   Goddam it.

> *LISE leaves. MICHAEL turns around.*

MICHAEL   Don't go.

MATHIEU   I have a mandate from the people of Quebec.

MICHAEL   You have an affirmative answer from 53 percent of the population of Quebec to a question that was three paragraphs long and still managed to be incredibly vague.

MATHIEU   Nonetheless.

MICHAEL   Look. Have a look at that file. Look what we will do to you.

MATHIEU   Are you prepared to engage in the massive constitutional reform necessary to keep Quebec in Confederation?

MICHAEL   In fact, there will be no constitutional reform. In fact, now that I think about earlier attempts at constitutional reform, we may even take some things back.

MATHIEU   Really?

MICHAEL   Really. Starting with that motherfucking notwithstanding clause. With the exception of friggin' Switzerland, this country has had the weakest federation on the planet for years, and look where that got us. But really, any discussion about our actual relationship, what it will actually be, is stupid right now. First, I have to make you want what I want. Once you do, all the other stuff will just happen.

MATHIEU   It would be treasonous for me to even enter into such a conversation.

MICHAEL   Ha ha, look who's suddenly concerned about treasonous behaviour. All right. I will show you something instead. It's eleven thirty now. Come to my hotel room at two o'clock. *(He tosses MATHIEU his room key.)* Please. Or we can start to have the conversation contained in that file, right now.

MATHIEU   I don't think I–

MICHAEL   Good. Two o'clock. Now please excuse us.

              After a beat, MATHIEU rises.

              Mathieu. Please understand, I don't know what I'm doing here. I'm not having a plan that you need to figure out.

MATHIEU   *That, I believe.*

MICHAEL   Please don't waste any time trying to decipher me. Just think about what I'm asking.

              He leaves.

              How's that for improvisation?

COLIN   You're a dead man.

MICHAEL	Well, yeah, but at least I'm not wasting your time anymore.
COLIN	Your career is over.
MICHAEL	So soon? I've only just figured out how to run the room.
COLIN	What gives you the right to set aside this government's carefully constructed plan and pursue this–
MICHAEL	Tell me you don't want this. Tell me you don't hope it's not too late.
COLIN	I don't. I do not hope. Hope is a fucking–, is not useful in this situation.
MICHAEL	You're probably right. And yet, there hope is, the fat, stubborn bastard, inelegant and inopportune. All sweaty and ready to kiss you full on the mouth, is hope. I'm gonna go talk to the press now, tell them the focus of the talks has shifted. Once it's in the paper, it'll take a day or two for our guys to figure out how to yank me off this. Don't get in my way.
COLIN	Whazzat?
MICHAEL	You heard me. Stay the fuck out of my way while I try and clean up your mess.
COLIN	Michael–
MICHAEL	Now this. This is FUN.

Blackout.

Scene Two

> *Music: Lullabye Baxter's "Mr. Powder-Blue Breadbox." Lights up on MICHAEL's room. He waits, then goes to the door and admits MATHIEU.*

> *As the music continues, MICHAEL ushers*
> *MATHIEU in, they speak briefly, and then*
> *MICHAEL takes off his pants. He seems to be*
> *encouraging MATHIEU to do the same.*
> *MATHIEU is reluctant. MICHAEL seems*
> *insistent. The lights fade down and the music swells*
> *up as MATHIEU begins to remove his pants, and*
> *MICHAEL reaches for the remote. Blackout. In the*
> *black, the music fades and we hear a couple of soap*
> *opera actors making their way through a torrid*
> *scene. The lights come up on MICHAEL's hotel*
> *room. MATHIEU and MICHAEL seated, pantless,*
> *watching TV. MATHIEU is bored almost to the*
> *point of implosion. He tries to watch, covering his*
> *wandering eye and leaning in with the good one.*
> *Finally:*

MATHIEU   Can we turn it off, now?

MICHAEL   Next commercial.

> *A pause.*

MATHIEU   Who the hell are these people?

MICHAEL   No no. Shut up. It doesn't matter.

> *A pause. More squirming from MATHIEU.*

Stop squirming. *(after some time has passed, while*
watching) You know, I read this thing once where a
fellow taped an entire day's TV, everything that
happened on TV in a single day, all the channels,
and then he sat down and watched it. Took him
months. Then, he went and he sat on a mountain
for twenty-four hours and he watched everything
that happened out there in nature, for a whole day.

And to be honest, I forget the point of why he did
that, but it made me think of something. It made
me think of how big this country is. Well, it made
me start to think about it. Because it's very big.
Very big. And most of it's outdoors.

MATHIEU	Uh huh.
MICHAEL	And I don't like the outdoors. Very much. I don't trust them. Do you?
MATHIEU	Do I trust the outdoors?
MICHAEL	Yeah. You're pretty much an urban fellow, right? Have you got a cottage, for instance?
MATHIEU	Yes I do.
MICHAEL	Is it drywalled?
MATHIEU	Uh, yes.
MICHAEL	So, there you go. It's not really a cottage. You're an indoor person, like most of us. But it didn't used to be like that. This is an outdoor country, and it used to be full of people who actually liked the outdoors. And they'd meet up, and look at each other, and they'd just know: "He and I both know what it's like out there. I got bit by the same bugs he did. I looked at the same rocks and trees as he did a few days ago. We both avoided the same bear."
MATHIEU	But now it's this?
MICHAEL	That's right. Now it's this. This is how we know how to talk to each other. The country is indoors now, and this is the country.
MATHIEU	But it's so awful.
MICHAEL	Sure, but the content isn't the point. The rocks and the water and the trees weren't the point then, for our large, smelly forefathers. The fact that you and I could be separately watching the same awful thing at more or less the same time, is. This is our wilderness. This is our shared… thing. Here we go.

The commercial comes and MICHAEL turns off the set. He blinks his eyes, gives his head a shake.

So? How 'bout it?

MATHIEU   How 'bout what.

MICHAEL   Staying.

MATHIEU   Based on that? Based on our shared dislike for the
            outdoors? Are you kidding me?

MICHAEL   No, based on the fact that we are essentially the
            same person.

MATHIEU   But we aren't.

MICHAEL   No, but we are.

MATHIEU   No we aren't.

MICHAEL   Well, yeah, we are.

MATHIEU   (Rapidly) *All right then, melonhead, if we are the same
            person, tell me what I'm saying right now. Open your
            mouth and make me believe you and I have anything at
            all in common. Go ahead.*

MICHAEL   Okay, now that's not fair. That's just language.

MATHIEU   Just language!

MICHAEL   Look, Mathieu. I like you. I'm starting to like you a
            lot. You're actually sort of a decent fellow.

MATHIEU   Thanks a lot.

MICHAEL   But look. There's nothing I can offer you to stay.
            I can't give you anything. And it's been proven that
            giving you things doesn't satisfy the thing in you
            that makes you want to go anyhow. I can't appeal
            to reason, because you aren't being driven by
            reason. I can't reverse the past, so I can't fix your
            grievances. The only thing I can do is try to change
            your mind. The only way I can think of to do that is
            to just sort of hang out with you. Unfortunately, our
            time is limited, because very soon they will figure

out a way to replace me and whoever replaces me will have a very different agenda.

MATHIEU   Michael, I like you. I don't understand you, but you are clearly being driven by something original, by something about which you have become passionate. I would go as far as to say I trust you. But there is nothing you can say that will make the slightest difference to me.

MICHAEL   Exactly. I agree one hundred per cent. It's the perfect place to start.

MATHIEU   Michael, I am very tired. Give me my country and let me go home.

MICHAEL   You are home.

MATHIEU   No, I'm NOT. Goddam it. How can you remain so wilfully ignorant?

MICHAEL   Look, if I don't intervene here, you'll walk out of these talks with a Quebec about a third of the size it is now, with chunks cut out of the leftover part, one of those chunks possibly being Montreal; you'll have to print up your own money starting like yesterday – you know, it'll be chaos.

MATHIEU   I'll handle it.

MICHAEL   Listen. I understand. You're a proud man. You're a proud people.

MATHIEU   What?

MICHAEL   But I have to believe you're also smart enough to realize when you're screwed.

MATHIEU   I'm not, will you stop–

MICHAEL   You had a good run at it. A great run. You got the people up, got them worked up and then all charging in the same direction. It was fantastic politics. You're a hero, really. To me. Don't tell anyone. But it's over. I'm telling you this as a friend.

The thing we need to do now is allow you to maintain a shred of dignity through the days and months to come. No reason why you need to go down when the whole separation thing caks. So you and I come up with a reason for Quebec to stay. And I still say television is the best place to look for that reason.

MATHIEU   Michael–

MICHAEL   Or, culture. Our shared, like, culture.

MATHIEU   What shared culture!

MICHAEL   Well, shit, I don't know. But listen, don't worry. By the time we're done spinning this, you can run that province as long as you like.

MATHIEU   How the hell do you – Why do you insist on misunderstanding the things that are happening around you? Why do you – *Will you never get it?*

Will you never get what is happening? *God. You're not even an adversary. You're a hindrance, like a, a charleyhorse or a blood clot or something.*

How could you.... *We've been engaged in this for so long, how can you remain so ignorant? My God. You know what? You should have kept us down. You should have kept us under your boot when you conquered us. You should have a–*

MICHAEL   Mathieu, slow down, I can't unders–

MATHIEU   *–you should have a goddam holiday every year to remind us we lost.* That would have been the humane thing to do. How could you.... *I have waited my entire life, I have been incredibly patient, we all have, and we try not to take each setback personally, try not to take them to heart.* Eventually we just stopped listening to you. *Because you say the wrong things. Always. You* *always say the wrong things. And when you say the right things, you still manage to do the wrong things anyhow.*

MICHAEL   Good, Mathieu. Let it out.

MATHIEU   Do you know, do you know, *I thought, I actually believed that this whole thing would drive me mad. I thought I'd go nuts, trying to get this very simple task done. Trying simply to formalize what has been our relationship for so long now anyway. Trying to get you people to just admit it. Just say it,* just once.

                            And it's not just you. *My own people threatened to drive me mad. I spent years giving my people the imagination to take the step, I learned, I had to learn how to impart courage—*

                            It's not in my nature, you know, that kind of public behaviour. I learned that. I artificially developed a persona people could attach themselves to.

                            I mean, you know what I'm like. It was agony to become someone people could stand being around, let alone actually like. Let alone actually believe in. Not that people like me, I know that. I don't need to be liked, I'll settle for being revered. I'll settle for getting this done.

MICHAEL   No, don't be so hard on yourself. I like you.

MATHIEU   And it is done. Now I can stop pretending you're evil and you can stop pretending I'm evil and we can start dealing with each other honestly. It's finally over. Or it would be, if you'd just cut this shit out and do what you're supposed to do. God, it's like you're genetically disposed to doing the wrong thing. Just do what you're supposed to do.

MICHAEL   I'm trying! I'm trying to help! They want to fuck you, remember? I'm putting everything at risk to keep them from doing that to you. I want to keep that from happening.

MATHIEU   You don't get it. You just don't get it.

MICHAEL   What. Tell me. What.

MATHIEU   You're supposed to do all those things. You're supposed to try to screw us. Do what you're supposed to, for once. Jesus!

MICHAEL   Wait a minute. What are you talking about?

MATHIEU   *Aw, you stupid* – I have a deal, okay? I have a deal with Gifford.

MICHAEL   You – what?

MATHIEU   Yes. You're supposed to try to take advantage, and then they step in. I have a deal with them.

MICHAEL   With – them?

MATHIEU   God, you people. You never do what you're supposed to. Yes. I have a deal with them. We are going to tie our currency to theirs, not yours. They are going to be the first to recognize us, they are going to provide stability for the first few years. But not until you try to humiliate us. Go back in the room and humiliate us, for God's sake.

MICHAEL   You – wow. You must hate us.

   MATHIEU fails to find an audible response to this.

   Well, I must say, I feel a bit of a patsy.

MATHIEU   Sorry.

MICHAEL   That's funny.

MATHIEU   What.

MICHAEL   Well, we have a deal with them.

MATHIEU   You – what?

MICHAEL   Yeah. Our deal was they were going to line up at the border, just to scare you and give us a little leverage.

MATHIEU   Oh my God.

MICHAEL   Yeah. Huh. Fuckin' Gifford, eh?

        A pause.

        What did you offer them?

MATHIEU   What did you offer them?

MICHAEL   Water.

MATHIEU   *(simultaneous with the above)* Water. Jesus Christ.

MICHAEL   And that's the guy you're climbing into bed with.

MATHIEU   I don't have a choice. It was the only way to get out intact.

MICHAEL   Yeah, I see. It was a nice move, actually.

MATHIEU   Thanks.

MICHAEL   But, listen. Give me a chance.

MATHIEU   What can you possibly – what are we going to do, watch more television?

MICHAEL   No. Probably not. I'll think of something.

MATHIEU   No you won't.

MICHAEL   I might. You don't know who you're dealing with here, mister. I can be very persuasive.

MATHIEU   I don't think I have the stamina to continue like this. I just want this to be done.

MICHAEL   Two days max. Then I get fired and the next guy in the chair will more than fulfill your wish to be humiliated. C'mon. You owe me that.

MATHIEU   Michael–

MICHAEL   Two days. *Forty-eight hours.*

MATHIEU   God. All right. Where are my pants?

> *They get up to retrieve their pants. MATHIEU stumbles putting his back on.*

MICHAEL   You okay?

MATHIEU   Yes. I just, I guess I'm just tired.

> *MICHAEL gets the Ritalin, shakes one out.*

MICHAEL   Here. These are great, I find.

MATHIEU   What is it? Isn't this the thing you take for your...?

MICHAEL   Yeah. I eat them like candy.

MATHIEU   Isn't it–?

MICHAEL   No no. It's mostly herbal.

> *MATHIEU swallows the Ritalin.*

> *(taking one himself)* Listen. We can do this. We can do a monumental thing. C'mere.

> *MICHAEL pulls MATHIEU into a hug. MATHIEU is stiff and unresponsive, but loosens up some in its latter moments. LISE unlocks the door and enters, witnessing the hug's conclusion.*

MICHAEL &
MATHIEU   *(separating)* Oh, hi there, c'mon, uh...

LISE   I can come back.

MICHAEL   No, no, we're done. *(to MATHIEU)* Can we talk later? She and I are just gonna do some stuff, and then, can we talk later?

MATHIEU   In the morning?

MICHAEL   Well, I don't have a lot of time. How 'bout later tonight.

MATHIEU   Well–

MICHAEL   Great. I'll call.

MATHIEU   Oh, fine.

> *MATHIEU heads for the door.*

MICHAEL   Oh, and Mathieu. Let's not do anything about the water, and our friend, for the moment. If you won't, I won't.

MATHIEU   All right.

MICHAEL   Thanks. See you later.

> *MATHIEU exits. LISE and MICHAEL stand very far apart. A pause.*

LISE   What water?

MICHAEL   That's interesting.

> *A pause.*

Hello.

LISE   Oh, no you don't.

> *A pause.*

I'd like to punch you in half.

MICHAEL   By which I take it to mean you're giving serious thought to what I said before.

LISE   I don't even know what you said. I mean, what WAS that?

MICHAEL   I thought I was pretty clear–

LISE   You just, you have a totally wrong notion of what
            this is. It's quite delicate, and, and, and, there are
            rules, okay? That we agreed to. Fuckhead.

MICHAEL   You've spent too much time in a room with Colin.

LISE   Like, what is it you had in mind. What. Like did
            you have in mind like a girlfriend or something?
            Because it's just the stupidest thing to imagine,
            me like that. I'm forty-seven years old, me, you
            stupid–. And what, I just give up my whole,
            everything? Eh? Don't you know who I am?

MICHAEL   Yes.

LISE   Don't you see what I'm doing here? I'm needed.

MICHAEL   You are.

LISE   I mean, what about your wife.

MICHAEL   What about your husband.

LISE   I DON'T HAVE A HUSBAND.

MICHAEL   Since when.

LISE   Since the divorce two and a half years ago. Read
            a fucking newspaper. Me, I'm done. You have a
            family. You think I want to be responsible for–

MICHAEL   Lise. You just have to say no.

LISE   I KNOW. DON'T YOU THINK I KNOW?

            A pause.

            Jesus Christ. Can I have a drink?

MICHAEL   Sure.

            Nobody moves.

LISE   Do I have to get it myself?

MICHAEL   Would you mind? You're sort of scaring me.

                    LISE makes a drink.

LISE   And what the hell was he doing here?

MICHAEL   Oh. Mathieu and I have taken our relationship to a new level. I've asked him to stay.

LISE   You've what?

MICHAEL   I've asked him to reconsider your province's departure from Confederation.

LISE   You're kidding.

MICHAEL   Nope.

LISE   And is he?

MICHAEL   Well, yeah.

LISE   He wouldn't do that. Why would he do that?

MICHAEL   Well, I can be very persuasive.

LISE   Oh, shut the fuck up. It would be treason for him to consider it.

MICHAEL   You know, you can't actually commit treason if the country doesn't exist yet. But let's talk about us.

LISE   Okay. Look–

MICHAEL   Not here. And not actually talk. Let's go get something to eat.

LISE   Oh. All right.

MICHAEL   And then I'd like to engage in the most erotic public event I can think of: I'd like to take you shoe shopping.

LISE   Fine.

MICHAEL   But first, let's dance.

LISE   Yes, sure, why not.

They dance.

MICHAEL   This, I feel, is the best way to discuss this.

They dance some more.

MICHAEL   So. You're not married anymore.

LISE   No. Is that a problem for you?

MICHAEL   I guess not. I just, I sort of thought we were getting off on an equal footing there.

The phone rings, and they stop. Nobody moves. Eventually, the ringing stops.

Let's go.

LISE   Michael–

MICHAEL   Nope. Let's go.

They leave.

Blackout.

SCENE THREE

The ballroom. Night. COLIN comes in, wearing pajamas. He sits in the low light, in his place.

COLIN   Uh, I'm assuming you people can hear me.

It was me and my kind that did this.

Can he be right about that? I mean, he's mostly an asshole. Because all this time, all I ever tried to do

was to fix things. All I ever wanted was for us to…
well, you know.

Eventually, I forced myself to stop wanting it.
I used every outrage to purge myself of you. And
I had finally done so. This last time around was the
charm.

I was finally, finally cold. Then he said: don't go.
Don't go, that's all.

And it all came back, as though the last 37 years
had not happened. As though no purge had
occurred.

And my first thought was: no, I can't. Please don't
make me want to again. I can't. But I find, I do. For
fuck's sake.

A pause.

Sixteen years ago, sorry about this, but: sixteen
years ago I was home, it was spring, very wet,
and Natalie was out. I came in, she wasn't there,
I waited, and she didn't come home. I thought: did
she tell me about some thing she had? And then, it
got later and later and I thought: well, SHE'S out
late. You'd think I'd remember her saying she was
going to be out this late. And the later it got, the
more the whole thing seemed to unravel. Our
whole… thing. Until I thought: That's it. She left.
She's gone. And I began to rack my brains to figure
out why she left.

And I'm a bright guy, I figured it out. I imagined
what I was like for her, married to me, how awful
it must be to be bound to a guy like me, never
around, never available, even when I was home.
I became amazed she'd stayed with me as long as
she had. I decided really, it was the only reasonable
thing for her to do, leave. And so when she walked
in, came back from whatever thing it was she had
overnight somewhere, I had to act like I hadn't

even noticed. I was shaking, and I said "Oh, were you gone?"

In one night I got to see how thin the thing we stand on is. The agreement you make. So.

A pause.

Okay. It was me and my kind that did this. Okay. Fine.

Here's what I did. It might help if someone says it all, once. I'll set it all out. And I'll do it in an way even you people can understand. So listen up, I'm only going to do this the one time. And I'll deny I said it.

It was me and my kind that did this. Okay.

In 1713 they gave us Acadia. And I got rid of the Acadians right away.

And then in 1760, Montreal fell to me, and of course I began putting up signs in English right away.

Then, the cocksucking *Americans*—how do you people get by without decent swear words?—*they get independence, and I pour over the border, packs of me, because I don't feel like being* cocksucking *Americans. I'd rather come up here, sit on you people for a while.*

Then what was I doing?

Lights start to fade on COLIN.

Oh yeah, I wrote this report, not one of my better moments, it said it was only a matter of time before I ate you alive.

I don't know what was in my head, I think I thought you couldn't read or something. Anyway, *that's probably what saved you, saved it from happening, my writing that and you getting your hands on it.*

Then what?

Blackout.

SCENE FOUR

> *MICHAEL's hotel room. MICHAEL on the couch,*
> *the TV tuned to a Quebecois station. LISE lies across*
> *the couch, her feet on MICHAEL's lap. They have*
> *had dinner, they have had sex. She wears two*
> *different, fabulous, shoes. Shoe boxes and Holt*
> *Renfrew bags all around.*

MICHAEL   See, here it is. Here's why we will never get along. Your TV is incomprehensible.

LISE   Answer the question.

MICHAEL   Like, who is that guy? Is he some sort of talk-show host? Why does he have that wig on?

LISE   He's, well, he's sort of an interviewer.

MICHAEL   Really?

LISE   Answer the question.

MICHAEL   Look at him. Jesus. Why is he standing on his desk? You see why we find you so mysterious.

LISE   *(turning off the TV)* It's very significant, your refusal to answer the question.

MICHAEL   I'm not refusing, I'm stalling. Uh, let me see. Well, I guess I want to be the Prime Minister mostly because a bunch of very pushy guys say that if things go well, I can have the job. And resisting those guys would seem to take more energy that not resisting them.

LISE   Nothing about the job itself?

MICHAEL   Oh, no, sure, the job is great. Do you know what the job description is? The job is reading.

LISE   Reading.

MICHAEL   Sometimes you read out loud, in front of people; sometimes just at a desk by yourself; occasionally you have to memorize something you've read and say it out loud; but that's pretty much it. Plus photos. The worst thing about being in cabinet is having to develop policy; there's none of that nonsense by the time you get to be PM.

LISE   Wow.

MICHAEL   I know. Now let me ask you a question.

LISE   Okay.

MICHAEL   Why do you ask.

LISE   Why do I...?

MICHAEL   Ask, yes.

LISE   Well. Because I'm trying to get to know you, I suppose.

MICHAEL   By asking about my job? Holy cow.

LISE   It can't be just a job. It must be who you are, at least a little bit.

MICHAEL   I promise you that you're getting all the useful information about me just by sitting here. It's happening without our doing anything about it. It's taking care of itself. My God, talk is so overrated. It's the worst way of doing anything. Talk, do you know what talk is? Talk is the enemy.

        A pause.

LISE   Tell me, Michael. What do you want.

MICHAEL	What do I…? What does anybody want. Lots of things, I suppose. Lots and lots.
LISE	What do you want out of this.
MICHAEL	Yes. I don't know.
LISE	No, listen. I have to know. I'm scared, okay?

> *MICHAEL gets up and finds the Ritalin, shakes out a couple of tablets.*

And your leaving the couch at this moment doesn't help, just for your information.

MICHAEL	Sorry. I'm stalling.

> *A pause.*

Sorry.

> *A pause.*

Have you ever seen me during question period?

LISE	Yes. Stick to English.
MICHAEL	Ever seen me do that thing where I talk before I know what I'm going to say? Where I jump up and get into a paragraph-long sentence before my brain engages?
LISE	It's a helluva skill.
MICHAEL	Well, listen. I could start talking now, and by the end, your fear will have diminished. I can guarantee that. Either that, or you'd be so worn out that your fear would seem diminished. But I find I don't want to. I want your fear. Look: there are so few palpable things. So few things that I don't have to fabricate and maintain on a minute by minute basis. And this *(He motions between the two of them.)* has its own, delicious momentum. And so I won't do it, I will not put my awful lying

mouth on any of this, not your joy, not your worry, not your fear or mine. I won't.

LISE   Your fear? What can you be afraid of.

MICHAEL   What am I–? Well, I'm not sure that's any of your business.

LISE   Of course it is. You're scared, I'm scared, and we feel like that separately, and I say, let's feel like that together.

MICHAEL   Ha ha, sure, but, I'm not sure we're well enough acquainted.

            A pause.

LISE   Please.

MICHAEL   Lise. Goddam it.

LISE   Tell me.

MICHAEL   All right. I suppose you're entitled to–. But. Um, you're not allowed, you can't say anything afterwards. Okay?

LISE   Sure.

MICHAEL   Boy, this goes against every single instinct I have about us.

LISE   Tough shit.

MICHAEL   Boy. Boy oh boy. All right. Well. Fuck. Look. I… could be anyone. Literally. There's no there there. You know?

            LISE nods.

            I know, I know, it's my greatest asset. It's the single greatest quality in a leader. But. It makes me… I'm… I normally don't mind. But I hate that that's what you see when you look at me. It's awful that you have to look at me. You see, I can't believe that, given that, that you're here at all.

LISE nods. A pause.

Say something.

A pause.

LISE   What do you think of these shoes.

MICHAEL   Yes. Good. I think they're astounding.

LISE   And you'd be right.

MICHAEL   There's so little actual shoe, and yet they seem so…

LISE   Substantial.

MICHAEL   Yes.

LISE   Yes.

MICHAEL   Yes. Good. Thanks.

A pause.

LISE   Is it time for you to call Mathieu?

MICHAEL   Yes. Probably. Yes.

He goes to the phone, dials. LISE regards him as the lights fade down

Blackout.

SCENE FIVE

Back to COLIN, still in the negotiating room.

COLIN   …got caught banging every single member of the Rolling Stones. So it was said. *Anyway, after that, you got all worked up, and I showed you. I walked right*

over to your place, kicked everybody off the streets.
I showed you. I kicked your ass. You killed a guy, but.
I kicked your ass.

Then you asked yourself, not me, but yourself, if you
should go. For the first time. And you answered yourself:
I dunno.

I, of course, said: don't go. And you said: why not. And
I said: I dunno.

So that went great.

And it wasn't long before the others pricked up their
ears. By then, we couldn't have a conversation anymore,
there were so many others in the room.—the fuckers—
"If you give them this, then we want that." *We'd*
never get a moment to ourselves again.

And then what. *Oh, I pulled some more shit, and you*
asked yourself over and over to go or not, and the answer
was always the same. And Christ was it boring.

My God, they're bad at this, everybody thought.

And so we are. So.

> *MATHIEU enters, dishevelled and wired. He puts*
> *on the lights. COLIN holds up a finger to silence*
> *him.*

And maybe this is just me, but I always thought the
question should be, if you insist on asking one over and
over, I always thought it should be:

What will you do without your hate?

Mathieu. You're up late.

MATHIEU   Am I? Of course. Yes. Who were you…?

COLIN   Nobody. The room. Never mind.

MATHIEU   Has Michael come in?

MICHAEL   Were you expecting him?

MATHIEU   I, yes, we just talked on the phone. He said to meet here.

COLIN   Really. Does he know what time it is?

MATHIEU   Does Michael know what time it is? I don't…. That's a hell of a question. Let's ask him when he comes.

COLIN   *(regards MATHIEU carefully)* Okay.

MATHIEU   Hey, but, what time is it?

COLIN   Well, it's pretty late.

MATHIEU   And you're here. Which is funny. Hey. Where's Michael?

COLIN   That's right. Are you okay?

MATHIEU   Well, I feel okay.

COLIN   Alrighty.

        A pause, MATHIEU walks around the room.

MATHIEU   *(more or less to himself)* What will I do without my hate. Yes. Ha ha.

        He walks around some more. Finally, MICHAEL enters. MATHIEU crosses to him and shakes his hand.

        Hey! Hi! How are ya!

MICHAEL   I'm fine. Hello, Colin.

COLIN   Michael.

MICHAEL   Nice jammies.

COLIN   Awright, fuck off, I just–

MICHAEL   No no, it's good you're here. *(to MATHIEU)* Did you get some rest?

MATHIEU   Well, I, actually, I watched some television.

MICHAEL   You did.

MATHIEU   Yes, several hours of television. It was fascinating, after a while. I'm beginning to understand its appeal.

MICHAEL   Tremendous. What did you watch?

MATHIEU   No idea. Do you have any more of those pills? They were great.

MICHAEL   No, but I can get some.

MATHIEU   Great for providing focus.

LISE comes in with several Holt's bags.

MICHAEL   I thought you were going to bed.

LISE   Not me. Colin.

COLIN   Madame Frechette.

MICHAEL   Well, great. Shall we?

All sit.

MATHIEU   So?

MICHAEL   So?

MATHIEU   So...

MICHAEL   Changed your mind yet?

MATHIEU   Michael. In spite of the fact that you seem to be right about television, I am not moved by that to throw over Quebec's nationhood.

MICHAEL	Well, can you think of any reason why you might change your mind?
MATHIEU	I'm supposed to do your job, too?
MICHAEL	Try not to think of it like that.
	A pause.
COLIN	Well. The talks proceed at a blistering pace. *(to MATHIEU)* HEY. *What will you do without your hate?*
MATHIEU	Yes, Colin. I was just thinking about that. I don't think I actually possess much hate anymore. But, it's interesting.
COLIN	It's interesting, you stupid fucker?
MICHAEL	Colin.
COLIN	You treasonous prick bastard?
MICHAEL	Colin.
COLIN	Arsewipe. Fuckhead. Pantywaist. Hey. Look at me. Look at me, Wall-eye.
MATHIEU	That's enough.
COLIN	Goddam right it's enough. It's a waste of my fuckin' time. What do you need. Like, what do you need? Is it an apology? Is it like, I dunno, a handjob and a kiss on the cheek?
MATHIEU	Yes, Colin. You're good at your job.
COLIN	No, fuck that. I've been at every one of these goddam meetings since the Plains of friggin' Abraham. I'm tired of this. Just say what you want. Christ, it's like you're the only one with anything to worry about. The only one who's had anything done to them in the history of the fucking world.

MICHAEL   Colin, this isn't productive, okay? Just–

COLIN   Productive. I've wasted my whole life, okay? Waiting to hear from him. I've never produced anything of value, of worth, IT'S ALL GONE, and this is how I'll be remembered: He fuckin' sat there while arsewipe here tore everything up. For what. FOR WHAT. For your ego, your little wounded self, you–. Goddam you.

Fuck it. *(rises)* Come here. COME HERE.

MATHIEU   What is he – hey!

COLIN   Fuckin' knock some sense into that French fuckin'–

MICHAEL   Colin! Enough. Sit down. Sit the fuck d–

COLIN   C'mere you fuckin' pussy. Kick your ass, AGAIN.

    Having circled downstage, COLIN lunges over the table at MATHIEU. MATHIEU retreats.

MATHIEU   You see? You see?

COLIN   What did we do? What did we do? Hey? HEY?

MATHIEU   Control yourself. Control him.

COLIN   If we did something, okay, we did something. I'm sorry for it, okay? Okay? I'm sorry for it.

MATHIEU   You're sorry? Is that right? You don't act sorry.

COLIN   Fuck, I'm fuckin' sorry, okay? C'mere and I'll show you just how fuckin' sorry I am.

MATHIEU   Ignorant redneck.

COLIN   Eh? Whazzat?

MATHIEU   You heard me. Fucking farmer.

    COLIN stops; is instantly calm.

COLIN   That's it. That's right. See? There you go.

             There's your hate. How long can you go without
             that? That's your affliction. It's not your fuckin' eye.
             That's your affliction. That's her affliction, that's his
             and mine. You live with that. It's you. You don't try
             to get rid of it. Then who would you be? Don't you
             know that yet?

MICHAEL   Are you out of your mind?

COLIN   Sorry, I was getting a little tired of all the talk. *(He
             sits.)* Fuck. I've got a knot in my chest a cannibal
             would spit out. Sorry about the language, Lisa –
             Lise. Fuck.

MATHIEU   Why do you persist, in the face of that? Even if you
             were able to change my mind, you could never
             change that. It would be simpler for all of us to just
             let this happen.

COLIN   Nobody said it was going to be simple, Monsieur
             Lapointe. Why do you want it to be simple?

MICHAEL   I'll start with you, then I'll worry about him.

MATHIEU   Michael, I don't even, what is it you want?

MICHAEL   I DON'T KNOW. Jesus. Why do people keep asking
             me that. But it just, it seems wrong, doesn't it? All
             these years, here, it's just been you and us, in this
             awful place, and we've made something work.
             Sometimes made something work. And you want
             to just, walk into the pitch black, just like that, stroll
             out there, and I, and you are my friend, okay, and
             I will not let you do that. I will not.

MATHIEU   This doesn't make–

MICHAEL   HEY. You are my friend.

MATHIEU   Don't yell at–

MICHAEL   YOU ARE. Tell me that doesn't matter.

MATHIEU   All right. Yes, you are, but–

MICHAEL   I have rights. As your friend.

MATHIEU   You...?

MICHAEL   I exercise those rights. Right now.

MATHIEU   What are you talking about?

MICHAEL   I don't know exactly. But I do. Right now.

MATHIEU   Michael, time's up. I'm genuinely sorry. This
             conversation is over.

MICHAEL   Mathieu–

MATHIEU   No.

              He heads for the Quebec door.

MICHAEL   *(to LISE)* Stop him.

LISE   Michael–

MICHAEL   Do it.

LISE   I can't–

MICHAEL   Hey. It's me. Do it. Do it do it do it.

LISE   *Mathieu, wait.*

MATHIEU   *(stopping)* Oh, God. WHAT.

LISE   Uh...

MICHAEL   Do it.

LISE   *Wait, okay? Just... just look at that man. Look at him.
             Uh, that man, that man has no discernible moral centre.
             He represents the worst of humanity, okay? He is a
             politician, in the foulest sense of the word. He is a man
             who would rather eat dinner with a foreign head of state*

> than have an idea. He wants to be Prime Minister, he
> doesn't seem to have a single reason for wanting it,
> beyond the vague notion it's an easy job. He is ignorant,
> willfully so, of our needs. He is a glorious example of the
> best reason to depart this federation. But I believe that
> in spite of his wretched, immature, criminally two-
> dimensional mode of living, in spite of his compulsions
> and petty needs and unconscionably simplistic view of
> his life and country, that he is owed something.

MATHIEU   *We owe him? We owe him what.*

LISE   *I don't know. Maybe just our attention. Maybe he should
be listened to, even if he says nothing. Even if it will
make no difference to what we will do. Even if it doesn't
count. Maybe he is owed our attention, in this instance,
to the point of our mutual exhaustion. Maybe the only
way to honourably do this is to keep going until we wear
each other out.*

MATHIEU   *I don't, I don't know. Why should I–*

LISE   *At least acknowledge that what we are asking for here is
the opportunity to become exactly like him.*

     A pause.

MATHIEU   *My God, will this never be over? (to MICHAEL)* Do
you have another one of those pills?

MICHAEL   No, but I'll happily get some. Will you be here
when I get back?

MATHIEU   I will.

MICHAEL   Good. Great. Won't be a minute. What were you
saying?

LISE   Oh, I convinced him of the worth of your character.

MICHAEL   God, you're wonderful.

LISE   I–

MICHAEL   Sorry.

LISE   No. It's okay. I admit it. I am.

           She kisses him, MICHAEL leaves. The three sit in
           silence briefly. COLIN gets up and moves away
           from the table, it sounds like he's attempting to stifle
           some laughter.

           Colin? What's so funny?

COLIN   No, nothing. Goddam it.

LISE   Share the joke.

COLIN   No, I… I'm not, there's nothing funny, really. I
           just…

           It's now evident that COLIN is actually weeping.

LISE   Are you all right?

COLIN   I guess I'm just tired. I, that was. You made him
           stay. She made you stay.

MATHIEU   Yes.

COLIN   Yes. You are still here. It's a gesture. It's the first one
           you've made in… I don't know. Sorry. *(He blows his*
           nose and laughs.) God. You people.

MATHIEU   I know exactly what you mean.

COLIN   I know. Fuck. I'm just so glad I'm here.

           The lights fade out. In the black, a telephone starts
           ringing. Lights up on MICHAEL's hotel room. He
           enters, looks briefly at the phone, and searches for
           the Ritalin. He finds the bottle, and stops once again
           to look at the phone. It stops ringing. The phone has
           killed his momentum, and so he sits on the couch.
           A pause with him seated, and then the phone begins
           to ring again. He picks it up.

MICHAEL   Hello? Hey! Hi. What are you doing up? What time
          is it? *(He checks his watch.)* Wow, it's really early, eh?
          How long have you been up? Really? Where are
          you. What are you watching? Uh huh. Wow. That
          sounds great, they, what, just turn into like a boat if
          they need a boat, or a – uh huh. Wow. No. I've
          never seen that one. Have I? We did? No, I don't,
          but if you say we did, then–
          When am I...? Oh, boy, I don't know. This thing, it
          was supposed to be just a couple of days, but now
          it's turned into a thing, a real big thing.
          Oh, no, it's all just really boring stuff. About the
          government, boring stuff.
          Really? What does she say about it?
          Really. Well, she's just being nice. It's actually not
          that–
          Really. Well, maybe she's right. It's nice of her to
          say. Will you thank her for me?
          No no, not now. It's too early. Let her sleep.

          A pause.

          Let her sleep. Sorry, what?
          No, what. Uh huh. Right. Ha ha. Uh huh. And then
          what. And then what, Franny. No, you said that
          part. You said that part, too – did the show just
          come back on? Do you want to hang up, now?
          Okay, Toots. I lo...

          *He hangs up the phone. After a long moment, he
          gets up, takes off his pants, sits back down, and
          reaches for the phone.*

          Blackout.

Scene Six

          *The ballroom, MATHIEU, LISE and COLIN.
          LISE is asleep on the table. MICHAEL enters,
          wearing a fresh suit.*

MATHIEU   Hey! What took you so long?

> *MICHAEL tosses the Ritalin to MATHIEU.*
>
> Thanks.

MICHAEL   Sorry, was I?

COLIN   Just about to send out a fuckin' search party. Let's go. Sit down.

MICHAEL   Will you wake her up, please?

COLIN   She's your girlfriend.

> *MICHAEL approaches LISE.*

MICHAEL   Lise? Lise?

> *After a beat, MICHAEL touches her.*

(softly) Mademoiselle Fréchette? We're ready to get started again.

LISE   Ah. *Yes. I... oh, it's you.* Oh. I'm sorry. Michael. I was having, you know that moment sometimes when you wake up and for a long, endless moment you don't know where you are, or who you are? Oh dear, I've drooled, I think. May I have your handkerchief?

MICHAEL   No, I, uh, I don't carry one.

COLIN   *(handing MICHAEL his)* Here.

MICHAEL   *Here.*

> *She wipes the drool from the front of her suit. She stops, and looks at MICHAEL.*

LISE   What did you say?

MICHAEL   I don't know.

LISE   What's wrong.

MICHAEL   Nothing, it's just, we need the, we could use the table.

> *He offers his hand to help her down. She does not take it.*

LISE   What's the matter?

MICHAEL   No. Nothing.

LISE   What is it?

MICHAEL   No, it's… *It's nothing. We talk later. We will talk later.*

LISE   Stop that. Talk about what.

MICHAEL   *Nothing, really, we will talk–*

LISE   STOP THAT. What is it. What. Say something.

MICHAEL   Not here. Not here, okay?

LISE   Not here.

MICHAEL   Let's talk, later.

> *A pause.*

LISE   You said no talking. Talk is the enemy.

MICHAEL   Lise.

LISE   We all know where talking gets us.

MICHAEL   Lise.

LISE   My God. That was fast, eh? You're fast.

MICHAEL   I–

LISE   I mean, it took me all this time to get there, to where I might seriously consider it, against my will, consider it, and then you're not there any more. You had the advantage, though. I mean, of course I was slower. I had to decide to be stupid.

> *LISE gets down by herself, stumbles on the*
> *mismatched shoes. MATHIEU moves to help her.*

LISE   And you. What water.

MATHIEU   Pardon?

LISE   WHAT WATER. What does he know that I–

MATHIEU   Lise, it was never my intention–

LISE   What did you do.

MATHIEU   I made a deal, a deal I had to make to insure we got what we worked for.

LISE   And he knows? And I don't?

MATHIEU   He forced me. I didn't want to, but he, he, he can be…

LISE   Yes.

MATHIEU   I'm sorry.

LISE   Me too. I'm going home.

MATHIEU   Lise, don't–

LISE   No. Listen. It's fine. You guys are made for each other.

> *She gives the handkerchief back to COLIN.*

COLIN   Lise. *I'm sorry.*

LISE   Not your fault.

COLIN   Well, yeah, he probably is.

> *LISE picks up some, but not all of the Holt's bags,*
> *and exits awkwardly through the Quebec door.*

COLIN   Come on. Let's go. Sit down.

MICHAEL   What? Oh, no Colin. No.

COLIN   Yes you will.

MICHAEL   No. Not me. Get somebody else.

COLIN   Yes, you. Yes you will.

MICHAEL   Colin. Don't–

COLIN   In the chair fuckhead. Do what you said.

MICHAEL   Colin–

COLIN   Sit. Down.

>   *A pause. MICHAEL sits.*

You too.

>   *MATHIEU sits.*

Right. Go. Don't go.

MICHAEL   Colin, don't be stupid.

COLIN   I'm not being stupid. You said it. It's what you want. So, go. It's all up to you. Right now. Go.

>   *A pause.*

MICHAEL   Mathieu, I'm sorry.

MATHIEU   You're sorry?

MICHAEL   Yes. Forget what I said.

MATHIEU   Forget what you...? You didn't say anything.

MICHAEL   That's right. Okay: You should know, Mr. Lapointe, I called our friend and he's decided to pull back the troops.

MATHIEU   You what?

MICHAEL	Yes. Basically told him to go ahead and drain the Great Lakes.
COLIN	Hey?
MICHAEL	Terrible deal for us. But with him out of the way, you've lost your leverage. It's just you and me.
COLIN	What?
MATHIEU	You said–. We had a deal.
MICHAEL	And I'll need those pills back. *(to COLIN)* It's okay. Go to bed. You're done. I got it.
COLIN	What do you mean.
MICHAEL	I'll do it.
COLIN	Do what.
MICHAEL	Nothing. What was asked of me.
COLIN	No. Don't do that. Do what you said.
MICHAEL	It's okay. You're done. You got me here. You're done.
COLIN	No.
MICHAEL	Colin. Please let me do my job. *(to MATHIEU)* So.
MATHIEU	Michael, please. How could you–
MICHAEL	No. I'm Mr. Fraser. And you're leaving. Let's go.
MATHIEU	But–. Where are we now?
MICHAEL	I have no idea. I don't think it matters.
MATHIEU	I… I need some. I'm not prepared at this time…
MICHAEL	Fine. Reconvene 10AM?

MICHAEL and MATHIEU stare at each other over the table. MATHIEU rises and leaves, leaving the Quebecois door open when he goes. COLIN looks at MICHAEL. He is incapable of speech, and suddenly very old. He gets up, goes to the Quebec door, carefully closes it, and he exits.

Music: "The Last of the Unplucked Gems", The Tragically Hip.

Blackout.

The end.